NEW DIRECTIONS FOR COMMUNITY COLLEGES

Arthur M. Cohen
EDITOR-IN-CHIEF

Florence B. Brawer
ASSOCIATE EDITOR

Directing General Education Outcomes

Neal A. Raisman
University of Cincinnati

EDITOR

Number 81, Spring 1993

JOSSEY-BASS PUBLISHERS
San Francisco

EDUCATIONAL RESOURCES INFORMATION CENTER

Clearinghouse For Junior Colleges

UNIVERSITY OF CALIFORNIA, LOS ANGELES

DIRECTING GENERAL EDUCATION OUTCOMES
Neal A. Raisman (ed.)
New Directions for Community Colleges, no. 81
Volume XXI, number 1
Arthur M. Cohen, Editor-in-Chief
Florence B. Brawer, Associate Editor

Microfilm copies of issues and articles are available in 16mm and 35mm, as well as microfiche in 105mm, through University Microfilms Inc., 300 North Zeeb Road, Ann Arbor, Michigan 48106.

LC 85-644753   ISSN 0194-3081   ISBN 1-55542-686-7

NEW DIRECTIONS FOR COMMUNITY COLLEGES is part of The Jossey-Bass Higher and Adult Education Series and is published quarterly by Jossey-Bass Inc., Publishers, 350 Sansome Street, San Francisco, California 94104-1310 (publication number USPS 121-710) in association with the ERIC Clearinghouse for Junior Colleges. Second-class postage paid at San Francisco, California, and at additional mailing offices. POSTMASTER: Send address changes to New Directions for Community Colleges, Jossey-Bass Inc., Publishers, 350 Sansome Street, San Francisco, California 94104-1310.

SUBSCRIPTIONS for 1993 cost $48.00 for individuals and $70.00 for institutions, agencies, and libraries.

THE MATERIAL in this publication is based on work sponsored wholly or in part by the Office of Educational Research and Improvement, U.S. Department of Education, under contract number RI-88-062002. Its contents do not necessarily reflect the views of the Department, or any other agency of the U.S. Government.

EDITORIAL CORRESPONDENCE should be sent to the Editor-in-Chief, Arthur M. Cohen, at the ERIC Clearinghouse for Junior Colleges, University of California, Los Angeles, California 90024.

Cover photograph by Rene Sheret, Los Angeles, California © 1990.

CONTENTS

EDITOR'S NOTES   1
Neal A. Raisman

1. Toward a Second Wave of Reform   5
Jerry G. Gaff
How can community colleges follow the university trend to redesign and refocus general education to meet learning needs?

2. The De Facto State of General Education   13
Neal A. Raisman
A study shows general education is not as well supported as it should and could be if appropriate steps were taken at colleges.

3. General Education in the Community College: 21
Developing Habits of Thought
Judith S. Eaton
Community college attendance patterns and part-time learners require a different definition and approach to general education.

4. Broadening Our Conception of General Education: 31
The Self-Regulated Learner
Claire E. Weinstein, Gretchen Van Mater Stone
General education can be used not only to teach but also to empower students to become expert learners.

5. Teaching Values Through General Education   41
R. Murray Thomas
Students need to be engaged in the process of forming values and thinking critically to become fully realized individuals.

6. Globalizing General Education: Changing World,   51
Changing Needs
Douglas P. Sjoquist
The rapid internationalizing of knowledge underpins curriculum changes such as the replacement of Western civilization with world civilization courses.

7. General and Developmental Education: Finding   59
Common Ground
Thomas L. Franke
Has developmental education become so prevalent in community colleges that it
should be considered part of general education?

8. General Education for At-Risk Students   67
Laura I. Rendón, Janyth Fredrickson
At-risk students have special needs for general education that must be met if
they are to succeed.

9. Vocational Education and General Education: 75
New Relationship or Shotgun Marriage?
James Jacobs
There are important ways to unite general education and liberal arts and prepare
students to enter technological careers.

10. General Education in Occupational Programs: 85
The Barriers Can Be Surmounted
Carole Finley Edmonds
Lessons from the Shared Visions Task Force can help increase communication
between and redesign courses to unite general and vocational education.

11. Sources and Information: General Education   93
in the Community College
Neal A. Raisman, Karin Petersen Hsiao
Current literature on general education in the community college is presented in
an annotated bibliography.

INDEX   103

EDITOR'S NOTES

General education in community colleges has increasingly become a focus of criticism of and challenges to the concept of the *comprehensive* community college. Whether community colleges will retain a full and supported general education mission leading to transfer or else function solely as training institutions is a central concern of this volume. Put succinctly, a growing question is whether or not community colleges are providing the necessary general education required to meet the needs and goals of the more than 54 percent of all college freshmen who begin their postsecondary careers at the nation's community colleges rather than at four-year institutions. Of additional concern is whether or not the nation's postsecondary general education needs and goals are being met in the community colleges.

Studies such as those by Brint and Karabel (1989) and Clowes and Levin (1989) have gone so far as to question the validity of community colleges as providers of much more than vocational training. Media reports about inner-city community colleges, such as in Chicago, have publicized what are construed as real concerns about community colleges as gateways to the future for minority students (see Zwerling, 1986). With a Ford Foundation grant, the American Council on Education sought to address the "failing transfer function." The keynote address at the 1990 meeting of the Liberal Arts Network for Development characterized general education in community colleges as failing to fulfill its goals and called for greater cohesiveness in the community college curriculum (Gaff, 1990). These are but a few examples of current concerns that focus on the general education curricula in community colleges and their ability to meet their identified objectives. General education is central to that function, and if it is not achieving its goals, the community college cannot meet its own broader goals. If the general education component of community college education is in disarray or incompatible with the higher goals of education and future student and cultural needs, then the current criticism is indeed fair.

Central to the concern is the continuing difficulty in operationally defining general education. Community colleges appear to have discussed general education as a concept and implemented curriculum programs labeled as general education even though there is no widely accepted definition. Mayhew's (1960, p. 9) statement that "general education is really a meaningless term since people define it in about any way their fancies dictate" still holds. General education programs and their objectives necessarily suffer from this inconsistency. This in turn has led to confusion over the state of general education since researchers have also worked from inconsistent definitions.

No prescribed or doctrinaire definition has been adopted by the contributors to this volume, Directing General Education Outcomes. It is hoped that the cumulative thought and expertise that they provide through the chapters will help lead community colleges to a unified definition and thus to adequate resolution of the problems that we face.

In Chapter One, Jerry G. Gaff reviews advances in general education reforms that generated a first wave of positive change. He then proposes specific steps to move into the next wave of reform needed to fully empower general education for community colleges.

If we are to determine a community college definition of general education, it will be necessary to understand the actual current condition of general education. In Chapter Two, I focus on research conducted in one state to understand the de facto condition of general education and the lessons to be drawn from this reality.

In Chapter Three, Judith S. Eaton suggests that general education must recognize the demographics of community college students, which indicate the need to move away from the mere learning of information and toward analytical and synthetic reasoning skills. She argues that we must develop "habits of thought" as a core for general education.

In Chapter Four, Claire E. Weinstein and Gretchen Van Mater Stone recognize that many community college students need to learn how to learn in order to become expert, self-regulated learners who can then become lifelong learners in the truest sense. General education for living in our society demands that educators move away from the simple transference of information and instead help students develop the ability to learn and understand values as a process of learning. R. Murray Thomas, in Chapter Five, develops specific approaches and exercises to teach values in the community college class.

In Chapter Six, Douglas P. Sjoquist reports on the need for general education to reach beyond local boundaries and to recognize that the definition of community is now international. Sjoquist discusses specific programs and techniques for internationalizing general education.

Has developmental education become a part of general education in the community college as a result of the weak basic skills and abilities of too many students? This is the question that Thomas L. Franke raises in Chapter Seven, where he provides models for bridging developmental needs with general education.

Do at-risk students need a different general education program from that of other students if they are to succeed and transfer? Laura I. Rendón and Janyth Fredrickson discuss this question in Chapter Eight.

In light of rapidly accelerating technological change, such as the computerization of industry, James Jacobs, in Chapter Nine, suggests that the traditional vocational education model for community colleges is in a profound crisis. He outlines six specific areas that a general education program must address to meet the needs of today's work force.

In Chapter Ten, Carole Finley Edmonds identifies areas where educators have achieved a consensus about the general education needs of occupational students and those where controversy exists. She makes recommendations to bridge the perceived gap between general education and occupational education for an integrated approach.

In Chapter Eleven, Karin Petersen Hsiao and I provide an annotated bibliography of current literature on general education in the community college. The resources listed cover general background on the topic and discussions of the relationship between general education and lifelong learning, the globalization of general education, and the role of general education in occupational and vocational programs.

Neal A. Raisman
Editor

References

Brint, S., and Karabel, J. *The Diverted Dream: Community Colleges and the Promise of Educational Opportunity in America, 1900–1985*. New York: Oxford University Press, 1989.

Clowes, D. A., and Levin, B. H. "Community, Technical, and Junior Colleges: Are They Leaving Higher Education?" *Journal of Higher Education,* 1989, *60* (3), 349–355.

Gaff, J. G. "Coherence in the Community College Curriculum." Keynote address presented at the annual meeting of the Liberal Arts Network for Development, East Lansing, Michigan, February 1990.

Mayhew, L. B. (ed.). *General Education: An Account and an Appraisal; A Guide for College Faculties*. New York: Harper & Row, 1960.

Zwerling, L. S. (ed.). *The Community College and Its Critics.* New Directions for Community Colleges, no. 54. San Francisco: Jossey-Bass, 1986.

NEAL A. RAISMAN is associate provost and special assistant for university planning at the University of Cincinnati, Cincinnati, Ohio.

Much has been accomplished in general education reform, yet much more is left to be done. Specific steps to lead community colleges into the next reform wave are considered.

Toward a Second Wave of Reform

Jerry G. Gaff

The United States is in the midst of an extended national debate about the quality of education. The debate is heated, even passionate, as fingers are pointed everywhere. The most generic issue in this debate, and the one thing on which all critics agree, is excellence. The gist of the matter is this: We are not doing well, and we can—and must—do better.

The focus of the debate, at least at the college level, is the curriculum. And within the curriculum, it is general education. The concern is not so much that students are not competent specialists in biology, sociology, literary criticism, computer operations, nursing, or other technical areas, for example. It is that they do not possess the marks of generally educated individuals, that is, "the knowledge, skills, and attitudes that all of us use and live by during most of our lives—whether as parents, citizens, lovers, travelers, participants in the arts, leaders, volunteers, or good Samaritans" (Association of American Colleges, 1988b, p. 3). In terms of the curriculum, general education is that portion studied by all students, regardless of their academic majors or intended careers.

The college curriculum, ideally, not only should be of high quality and possess rigorous content but also should be coherent. Unfortunately, community colleges, in pursuit of enrollment, have too often adopted "cafeteria" approaches to general education. Students have been able to select their own main courses, entrees, and condiments without regard for the "intellectual nutrition" required for a balanced education. As the Association of American Colleges (1985, pp. 2–3) has expressed, "The curriculum has given way to a marketplace philosophy: it is the supermarket where students are shoppers and professors are merchants of learning. Fads and fashions, the demands of popularity and success, enter where wisdom and experience should prevail. . . . The marketplace philosophy refuses to establish common expectations and norms. Another victim of this posture of irresponsibility is the general education of the American college undergraduate, the institutional course requirements outside the major. They lack a rationale and cohesion or, even worse, are almost lacking altogether. Electives are being used to fatten majors and diminish breadth. It is as if no one cared, so long as the store stays open."

One of the reasons for a lack of coherence has been pointed out by Virginia Smith (1989); she says general education seems to be more of a catalogue construct than a genuine academic program. Whereas the smallest academic department has a chairperson, a faculty, and a budget, similar accoutrements are absent from general education, even though its size and educational significance dwarf even the largest department. Decisions about courses, faculty staffing, and budget for general education are typically made by dozens of relatively autonomous departments. This arrangement virtually guarantees that the core curriculum will be fragmented and lack coherence.

First Wave of General Education Reform

A veritable reform movement took place in reaction to the debate during the last decade. Faculties on campus after campus reached agreement on the qualities of an educated person. They began taking steps to more intentionally produce those qualities by changing graduation requirements, the curriculum structure, individual courses, and teaching-learning approaches. Several trends can be identified in the community colleges, as well as four-year institutions, that have chosen to couple excellence with access.

Liberal Arts and Sciences Subject Matter. The liberal arts and sciences are the most fundamental and useful bodies of knowledge, methods, and perspectives devised by the human mind. Spurred by concerns for excellence, the arts and sciences are taking a more prominent place in the curriculum, even in professional and preprofessional programs.

Fundamental Skills. Skills such as writing, speaking, logical or critical thinking, foreign language, mathematics, and computing are given greater emphasis in modern curricula. Students are having their abilities assessed for success prior to enrollment in courses and programs.

Higher Standards, More Requirements. This trend, like the others, plays out in different ways at different institutions. More and more community colleges are placing entrance requirements on their courses. Assessment of skills and subsequent placement in courses are becoming the rule in many colleges. Degree and certificate programs with matriculation requirements, mandatory examinations for entry into upper-division study, and more specific graduation requirements are variations on the theme.

Tighter Curriculum Structure. The trend is away from loose distribution requirements that students may satisfy with any of a large number of courses. It is toward a more purposeful curriculum consisting of a limited set of courses that serves specific goals, common core courses for all students, or some combination of the two for the associate in arts and associate in science degrees, with increased general education requirements for associate in applied science and certificate programs.

Freshman Parallel Year. Freshman topical seminars, stronger advising, and more attention to intellectual and personal development are designed to introduce new students to college-level work.

Global Studies. Given the growing planetary interdependence of economic systems, environmental problems, and security needs, colleges are emphasizing the study of other cultures and peoples.

Gender and Ethnic Studies. Another trend is greater attention to cultural pluralism within the United States and the Western tradition, and the incorporation of the "new scholarship" on these topics in the core curriculum.

Integration of Knowledge. Integration is what is higher about higher education, according to Harlan Cleveland (1980). Thematic, interdisciplinary, and topical courses and programs are found in many revised curricula. Connected thinking is emphasized.

Moral Reflection. More than technical expertise is expected of an educated person, and colleges are reemphasizing values through the study of non-Western cultures, professional ethics, social problems, and the implications of science and technology.

Extension Through All Four Years. Rather than consisting only of introductory courses relegated to the first two years, new general education programs often include advanced courses and extend throughout the entire college career. Increasingly, community college graduates transferring to four-year colleges should expect to find that they have not completed all of their general education requirements.

Need for a Second Wave of Reform

Critics may charge that these changes do not go far enough, are not widespread enough, or are too superficial—in the incomparable words of Groucho Marx, "There is less here than meets the eye." But these reforms have changed the shape of the college curriculum. More can and should be done, but change is in process in many community colleges.

Despite the significant improvements that have been made, much more remains to be done to strengthen undergraduate education. At this time, we need a second wave of reform with new ideas and energy that can continue the spirit of reform through the 1990s. There is a need to extend the reforms to involve more colleges and to deepen the changes that have already been made.

The first wave has been dominated by concerns for content and changes in the formal curriculum. But as important as subject matter is, and it is essential, it is only one of the elements in the education complex. It is time to get beyond the content issue and to bring other elements into the debate. For example, students have been conspicuous by their absence in recent curriculum changes. The diversity in the community college student body may, at first, seem almost impossible to define in any unified sense. It is vital, however, to understand the diverse abilities, interests, life experiences, and learning styles of these students to engage them fully in the education process. Faculty members, with their diverse instructional purposes, teaching styles, attitudes toward students, and career goals, ideally should come together to further the instructional aims of the curriculum. And although learning is an individual activity, it is not a solitary one. It takes place in an environment that can either support or undermine even the best curriculum. All of these factors should reinforce the curriculum and collectively serve the instructional purposes of a college by reinforcing common education principles. How can we do this?

First, students must overcome "the bargain," that implicit understanding between students and teachers that pervades most courses. In the bargain, the teacher prepares a detailed syllabus, sticks to it throughout the term, makes assigned readings in the texts, tests the material assigned, and grades fairly. The students dutifully does the assigned reading, attends class, takes the tests, and expects a respectable grade. Students who keep their part of the bargain may be serious, and they may even make good grades, but they lack intellectual curiosity. They are following the rules rather than following their minds as they search for answers to questions that are of interest to them. They are essentially passive. Such students are learning to be functionaries who will fit into organizational slots rather than thinkers and leaders who take charge of their lives and decide how to define the various roles that they play. The "bargain" must be overcome if education is to amount to more than what Whitehead called "the accumulation of inert ideas."

Second, it is important to decide which goals to seek and for teachers to have a pedagogy appropriate to achieving them. The simple typology offered by Russell Edgerton (1987), president of the American Association for Higher Education, is helpful. If our objective is to transmit information and knowledge, it makes sense for professors to tell students what they know, via the lecture format. But if, for example, our objective is to enable students to develop the ability to write clearly, analyze issues thoroughly, or think creatively, the lecture is an ineffective format. Students learn about things by being told, they learn how to do things by doing them. To teach abilities, professors must design tasks and create conditions in which students can learn by performing; and professors can then comment on their performance as it goes along. If our objective is to teach attitudes and values, still other modes are required.

Students learn these personal qualities best by having new experiences, especially those that expose their own attitudes, allow them to encounter different views, and force them to reconcile conflicts in attitudes or values. Internships, study abroad, or collaborative work with a person with different values are valuable learning experiences. Observe that many of these opportunities for learning are beyond the classroom and require faculty to move beyond the familiar lecture.

Third, learning is an individual—not a solitary—activity. It works best in the context of a supportive community of learners. There is a large body of research documenting the educational impact of small, close-knit communities, of opportunities for continuing formal and informal contact among students and faculty, and of the significant educational role of student peer groups. By hitching these various forms of learning to the substance and skills of the formal curriculum, an overall climate of learning is possible.

In short, the second wave of reform should go beyond the formal curriculum and concerns for content, as important as these are. It should seek to involve students actively, support faculty in an effective pedagogy for their teaching and courses, and create an entire college culture that is more supportive of the purposes of general education.

The particular role of community colleges can be examined in this context. Although community colleges are involved in the debate and are making improvements in their programs, they are underrepresented in the reform movement. Indeed, a few of their leaders react to discussion of a second wave of reform by remarking that the first wave is just hitting the beach at their institutions. Community colleges must play a central role in the second wave, in part because they enroll more than half of all freshmen and sophomores in the country. The quality of higher education, and of general education in particular, can be no better than its offerings in community colleges. If they are to achieve their potential in this regard, they will have to make several adjustments in their self-concepts and operations.

Traditionally, community colleges have stressed access, especially for those groups underrepresented in four-year colleges: individuals seeking vocational certification, adults, and ethnic minorities. They "save" a large number of at-risk students, those who often are less socialized into the habits and skills associated with college achievement and who have not been well served by the primary and secondary schools. These individuals possess enormous potential, and it is imperative that they have education opportunities. But it is necessary to stress quality as well as access. Unless colleges offer a quality education, the promise of access is empty. Robert McCabe, president of Miami-Dade Community College, argues that it is necessary to guarantee quality in order to keep the open door open (McCabe, 1982). The public simply will not support second-rate education. Access to quality is a winning formula.

Community colleges have a crisis of mission. They have neglected the transfer function, which always was a central part of their rationale. Alison Bernstein (1988) wrote that in California "of the more than one million community college students in that state's 106 two-year institutions, only 50,000, or about five percent, had transferred to four-year institutions." Aspirations seem to fall during the time that students spend in their community college programs. The collegiate function needs to be reasserted. Students, and the public, want community colleges to truly be colleges.

Community colleges have been market responsive, and they have been very creative in offering courses wherever there are enough students. This has been an appropriate strategy for new and expanding institutions. Now it is time for faculty and administrators to define, expound, and defend sound education principles, reasonable requirements, and standards of achievement to "educate the market" about what a college education is and can do—even at the danger of turning away a few students. In fact, students today find high standards attractive. More than one college has adopted more rigorous and coherent curricula only to see increases in applications, retention rates, and overall enrollment. Hamline University in Saint Paul, Minnesota, for instance, when I was the academic dean, adopted a more rigorous and tightly structured core curriculum. In three years, the applications increased over 50 percent, and the average American College Test scores are two full points higher. At Tougaloo College, a historically black college in Mississippi, former president Herman Blake discovered that the basketball team was not performing academically; he cancelled the rest of the season (Blake, 1989). That was taken as a sign by people all around the region that the college was serious about academic quality, and enrollment spurted 30 percent. Miami-Dade defined and then instituted and enforced clear standards, winning the respect of its students in the process (McCabe, 1982). If market-sensitive institutions declare what they stand for, they may make the pleasant discovery that students want colleges to place appropriate instructional demands on them.

Community colleges have traditionally served large numbers of vocational students. This is wholly appropriate. But in many colleges, occupational and technical programs have overwhelmed the liberal arts. It is time to reassert the importance of the liberal arts, even in vocational programs. The liberal arts are practical arts; they contribute to vocational and professional success. The Association of American Colleges (1988a) illustrated how this reemphasis can be accomplished through academic advising and trench warfare in conveying the value of the liberal arts curriculum. Communication skills, critical thinking, historical perspectives, social analysis, and moral reasoning are important in all careers.

It is important that faculty members and administrators help students see that they will be short-changed if they fail to acquire these skills and values. And students must also convince themselves, perhaps by reviewing their own preparation for their careers. There is one other practical reason for infusing the liberal arts throughout occupational and technical programs. Many, often most, of the students who transfer to four-year schools come from these technical programs. Moreover, today's jobs require increasingly more intellectual flexibility as technology demands workers who not only can perform a task but also can think and communicate.

Community colleges typically model their curriculum after the local state college, which is their larger receiving institution. This approach is understandable given that many of the students must have their courses accepted for transfer there. But the approach is also partly responsible for a "minimalist" view of what is expected and possible in general education. For example, a traditional discipline-based distribution scheme at the state college may constrain the development of a distinctive program, interdisciplinary offerings, skill-intensive courses, or other innovative instruction at the community college. Two-year colleges should raise their sights and model themselves on the best programs and institutions in the country. Then they should use their leverage as an important source of students to stimulate more creative thinking about general education in four-year institutions. The local state college will accept transfer students simply because it cannot afford not to, particularly as the potential student pool continues to shrink.

Conclusion

It must be acknowledged that there are many impressive programs operated by community colleges. Los Medanos College, in Pittsburg, California, has a distinctive three-tier program featuring a two-semester interdisciplinary sequence called Ethical Inquiry into Societal Issues, which focuses on topics such as equality, population, and the environment. LaGuardia Community College in Long Island City, New York, operates annually several thematic clusters of three related courses for liberal arts and business students, and these are powerful learning communities. Oakton Community College, in Des Plaines, Illinois, has established an honors program for part-time, evening, adult students. Rochester Community College in Minnesota works closely with Winona State College to allow students to take courses concurrently on the Rochester campus. This 2 + 2 model is being seriously considered for replication throughout the Minneapolis-Saint Paul region. These are all important new ventures, and more examples could be cited. But the point is that even more must be accomplished if students are to receive the very best general education that can be devised.

America is looking to the leaders of community colleges to join in the debate about quality and coherence in undergraduate education. If access is to lead to excellence, it must be joined to a coherent, general education core. If community colleges are to fully achieve their potential for our society, for themselves, and for their students, they need to place general education at the center of their definition as colleges.

References

Association of American Colleges. *Integrity in the College Curriculum: A Report to the Academic Community.* Washington, D.C.: Association of American Colleges, 1985. 62 pp. (ED 251 059)

Association of American Colleges. *An Engineering Student's Guide to the Humanities and Social Sciences.* Washington, D.C.: Assocation of American Colleges, 1988a. 32 pp. (ED 299 932)

Association of American Colleges. *A New Vitality in General Education: Planning, Teaching, and Supporting Effective Liberal Learning by the Task Group on General Education.* Washington, D.C.: Association of American Colleges, 1988b. 64 pp. (ED 290 387)

Bernstein, A. "Community Colleges: Coming of Age." *Change,* 1988, *20* (1), 4.

Blake, H. Panel discussion on "Issues in Higher Education: Diversity." Conference on Leadership in the Twenty-First Century, Depauw University, Greencastle, Indiana, April 1989.

Cleveland, H. "Forward to Basics: Education as Wide as the World." *Change,* 1980, *12* (4), 18–22.

Edgerton, R. Paper presented at the annual meeting of the American Association for Higher Education, Chicago, March 1987.

McCabe, R. "Excellence Is for Everyone: Quality and the Open Door Community College." Paper presented at the annual meeting of the American Association for Higher Education, Washington, D.C., March 1982.

Smith, V. "General Education: A Question of Purpose." Paper presented at the Council of Independent College Deans Institute, San Francisco, November 1989.

JERRY G. GAFF is director of the Project on Strong Foundations for General Education at the Association of American Colleges, Washington, D.C. He is the author of New Life for the College Curriculum: Assessing Achievements and Furthering Progress in the Reform of General Education *(Jossey-Bass, 1991).*

Discussions on general education have suffered from a lack of definitions and specific details from research. A study of the actual offerings in the state of Michigan's twenty-nine autonomous community colleges provides statistical details indicating the actual state of general education in Michigan and, through correlations, nationally.

The De Facto State of General Education

Neal A. Raisman

General education in community colleges has not undergone enough systematic scrutiny. If community colleges are to understand the strengths and weaknesses of their general education offerings, they must work from a factual, not inferential, base. A study of the fall 1989 course offerings of the twenty-nine community colleges in the state of Michigan was conducted in an attempt to determine the de facto condition of general education within community colleges (Raisman, 1990). Michigan was chosen since the twenty-nine two-year colleges are all autonomous of any centralized governing board or regents. Thus, the schools were free to determine and establish their own missions as well as the programs and curricula to carry out those missions. For example, based on their own, individual determinations of what general education should be, they have implemented changes to achieve their identified goals in this area. Moreover, the twenty-nine two-year schools all define themselves as comprehensive community colleges. They are not locked into a specific type of course or program offering as they might be if they were specifically vocational or technical colleges. If they emphasize offerings in any one area, it is not because they had to do so to meet a specific defined focus but rather because they made a decision to do so.

Basic Approach and Methodology of the Michigan Study

The definition of general education for the Michigan study was the same as that employed in Cross and Fideler's (1989) Community College Goals Inventory (CCGI) study. This definition was chosen since, in addition to providing a clear functional characterization of general education, it allowed for potential cross-correlation of results to an existing data base. Additionally, although the definition did not include all of the course offerings in the Center for the Study of Community Colleges (CSCC; 1978, 1982) and Cohen and Brawer studies (Cohen, 1988; Cohen and Brawer, 1987), the basic approach and methodology of the CSCC studies were used. Course offerings, rather than course credit or enrollments, were counted. The offerings were chosen since they indicated what each college chose to provide to the students rather than what the students chose to take, which would have generated a study of student preference rather than of institutional emphasis. The particular courses and the number of sections per course and program that a college offers indicate where the college places its emphasis since each offering must be supported with space, personnel, and administrative effort, all of which translate into budget and priorities.

The major points of difference between the Michigan study and the CSCC studies were the way in which courses were counted and which disciplinary areas were included. The Michigan study focused on general education offerings, so it did not count as general education the courses that had at least some liberal arts emphasis but were designed primarily to meet the specific needs of a vocational or technical program. For example, courses such as Technical Math, Writing for Business, and Physiology for Nursing Majors were not counted as general education course offerings. These courses were circumscribed in their scope, subjects, and areas to fit within specific curriculum emphases and thus were too limited to be general. These were considered career offerings and so were not counted. Additionally, the CSCC studies included agriculture and engineering as liberal arts, and thus, to some extent, general education areas. The Michigan study rejected these areas as specifically applied technical and vocational offerings and thus not general education

The results of the study of the 22,931 sections offered in Michigan in the fall term of 1989 indicated that the colleges chose not to emphasize general education. Discussions with college officials and initial surveys indicated that even though the primary instructional and student services officers believed that the schools were emphasizing transfer and general education, the reality did not match the assertion. A survey was sent to four administrators at each of the twenty-nine colleges: the chief instructional administrator and the deans of liberal arts, career education, and students. These surveys were reviewed for each college as well as totaled for the state. In many ways, the comments and assertions of the Michigan community college administrators surveyed reflected a dissonance similar to what Cross and Fideler (1989) found between what should be and what was actually the case. The survey results also indicated that the administrators believed that their colleges offered more general education than was actually disclosed by the study.

The study categorized the course offerings into one of five groupings:

(1) general education, (2) career education, (3) remedial and developmental studies, (4) physical education, and (5) community service and personal growth. The general education offerings were further broken into major curriculum areas, then into disciplines, and finally into subdisciplines. These discipline categories attempted to follow the CSCC patterns, but, as mentioned earlier, some CSCC categories were rejected and others were redefined or necessarily divided into more discrete categories to form subcategories, for example, minority and women's studies, film, and linguistics. The category into which a specific course offering was placed was determined by the course description in the college's catalogue, its placement within specific curricula, and, when necessary, review with an appropriate instructional officer at the college. An additional check on classification was done against the 1989–1990 Michigan Department of Education *Activity Classification Code Report of Public Community and Junior College Taxonomy/Student and Course Data.* This report is submitted by the individual colleges to the state to classify course offerings of each college for funding purposes. The report indicates the category into which the college places a course, that is, remedial, technical, general education, and so on. Admittedly, there was some blurring of distinctions, particularly in determining whether a course offering was for community service needs or physical education. For example, colleges offered sections in aerobics or swimming that could either fall into a physical education program or could have been provided as a community service. These classification questions did not have any effect on the general education offerings.

Results of the Michigan Study

The overall distribution of offerings is shown in Table 2.1. The results of the study indicated that out of the 22,931 course sections offered, only 7,006 or 31 percent were in nonremedial general education areas. Even with the addition of the 1,634 remedial sections offered into the general education category, the 8,640 sections equal 38 percent of all sections offered. The preponderance of the offerings were in career education. This category accounted for 12,488 sections or 54 percent of all of the course sections offered. Remedial and developmental offerings comprised 7 percent, while physical education equaled 4 percent, and community service and personal growth offerings equaled 4 percent.

Additionally, of the 7,006 offerings in general education, only 1,162, or 16.6 percent, could be classified as sequential follow-up courses that went beyond the introductory or survey course to focus on what is usually considered a major course of study. Thus, not only was the general education available to students in the twenty-nine community colleges extremely low in the number of course offerings in comparison to career education, it was also limited in the depth of knowledge provided toward a major concentra-

Table 2.1. Total Offerings and Percentages by Course Category

Area	Number of Sections	Percentage of Total
General Education	7,006	31
Career Education	12,488	54
Remedial and developmental studies	1,634	7
Physical education	861	4
Community service and personal growth	942	4
Total Offerings	22,931	

Source: Based on Raisman, 1990.

tion. In short, general education was a case of too little, spread too thinly. The CSCC (1982, p. 3) finding that "course offerings within disciplines also reveal that the Liberal Arts curriculum has a flat structure, characterized by an abundance of introductory survey courses and a relatively small number of more advanced courses at the sophomore level" reflects as well the general education offerings in Michigan. Twenty-four of the thirty-eight disciplines had only seven or fewer advanced, or major concentration courses statewide. Thirteen areas of study offered no follow-up courses. It would not be at all unfair to state that the community colleges were providers of introductory instruction with little advanced study to help students progress toward a major area of study.

These results correlate with the CSCC (1982) study, bringing additional credence to both studies while depicting what could be a troubling image for community colleges. Community colleges are providing for breadth, perhaps, but not for depth in many areas. This may not be a problem if that is what community colleges choose to do, but they do not appear to believe that they are limiting study to survey and introductory courses in general education and liberal arts areas. It may well be that an appropriate role for them is to provide introductory general education while leaving major area concentration to the receiving institutions. This approach would eliminate some of the transfer problems that students encounter when they attempt to transfer coursework beyond the introductory level. But an exclusive focus on introductory education would seriously impair the collegiate identity of community colleges.

Moreover, of the courses available in general education, the offerings in composition and mathematics were by far the most frequent in each school as well as statewide. There were 1,901 sections offered in mathematics and 1,770 sections in composition, for a total of 3,671 sections, or 42.8 percent of all general education offerings. These findings parallel those of the CSCC studies, wherein composition and mathematics constituted 41 percent of offerings and were the most frequent areas for offerings and enrollments.

These findings are not surprising since composition and mathematics are courses in service to other studies. The next highest number of sections offered was in political science, which provided 692 sections. This does not correlate with the CSCC studies and may not reflect a deliberate decision to emphasize political science courses. The high number of offerings may well be a remnant of a law in Michigan that called for the teaching of courses in American government or civics in the community colleges. The law was eventually rescinded, but the offerings remained in the catalogues perhaps for college or community political reasons or for enrollment purposes. It is also likely that the sections remained in the curricula simply because they had been there in the past and, out of neglect, no one had reviewed their current education purpose or objective. Since the courses were fully enrolled and were providing employment for instructors, why should administrators question them?

If the number of political science offerings is a remnant of the past, it reflects a larger problem for general education—inattention to educational and instructional concerns. The results of the survey suggest that administrative inattentiveness or, even worse, neglect may be a primary source of the de facto condition of general education. Although the sampling was not extensive enough to provide conclusive indicators, there is a basis for concern that the level of shared understanding of the reality of offerings and emphases on campuses is minimal. On some campuses, there were differences of perception on simple realities such as whether or not the colleges had a general education requirement and mandatory assessment and placement, as well as the percentages of students needing remedial work. For example, on three campuses, at least two of the four administrators per campus disagreed as to whether there was a general education requirement at their college. At four colleges, administrators split, two and two, on whether or not the college required assessment at entry. In response to the question "What percentage of students are assessed as being in need of remedial/developmental work in reading___, writing___, mathematics___?" administrators from the same college gave widely divergent answers.

For example, Table 2.2 presents the percentages reported by one set of deans at one college in response to the above question. The variations here indicate that these administrators are not in touch with one another on distinct educational concerns. They may also indicate that the college has not taken the remedial aspect of general education very seriously since it has not even determined the extent of the problem and disseminated the findings so that a consistent understanding can be obtained by all.

Remedial sections in reading, composition, and mathematics have been a consistent part of community college offerings. It is also worth noting the remedial offerings in some unexpected areas of study, such as foreign languages and the sciences. The twenty-two sections attributed to foreign language account for sections in English as a Second Language. This number

Table 2.2. Deans' Estimates of the Percentage of Students
in Need of Remediation in Basic Skills

Dean	Reading	Writing	Mathematics
Instruction	17	22	22
Arts and sciences	40	55	50
Career education	28	32	63
Students	35	35	35

Source: Based on Raisman, 1990.

might be seen as low in comparison to that found by CSCC (1978) or by Cohen (1988), but the general population demographics in Michigan can account for the lower number. Michigan is a state that has been seeing emigration rather than immigration, particularly among Spanish-speaking and Asian people. Moreover, the remedial courses and sections offered in chemistry, biology, and physics indicate that instruction in these sciences is lacking when students are not even prepared to take introductory studies in the sciences. This is an area in need of attention if instruction in science is to succeed.

What Needs to Be Done

What needs to be done in Michigan is really the same change that must occur nationally. A primary decision must be made on the nature of the purpose and role of general education in the community colleges. This is a decision that goes to the heart of the mission of community colleges. If general education is central to the mission, then the following steps should be taken.

First, colleges need to assess their actual offerings in general education. They should understand what they are actually doing and not what they say or think they are providing to students. The mission statement of too many colleges may be more of a wish list, or what has been called "the Seven Steps to Salvation," than a practiced reality. If there is a mismatch of mission statement to reality, one or the other will need to be reshaped.

An assessment of the de facto state of offerings not only will lead to a recognition of what is actually being offered on the campus but also will help focus attention on what general education, liberal arts, career education, and community service really mean in implementation. This assessment, and comparison to other colleges and other studies such as the one reported here, will allow an individual college to gauge how it compares to other institutions as well as to the perceptions of its own faculty and staff. With this understanding of where the college is actually placing its emphasis through offerings, the college will not only better understand its explicit, actualized definition but also review its implicit focus. Until a college knows what it is really doing, it will not be able to recognize who and what it really is. Without a real recognition of the actual state of offerings and emphasis, the college will not be able to redefine its future goals and meet them.

Second, administrators need to more fully comprehend what is occurring in their colleges and share that information with other administrators on campus. It is vital that a common reality be established between and through administrators. Administrators on the same campus must have a correct and consistent base of information from which their colleges can study and develop general education goals and programs. Without accurate knowledge, there is no way that administrators will be able to help their colleges mesh goals with future realities.

Third, once the actual condition of general education is determined, each college needs to decide whether it really wants to change its emphasis. If the college discovers, as was the case in the Michigan study, that the reality is not equal to the desire, it is necessary to evaluate the stated objectives. If general education is a goal worth pronouncing, then it must be supported.

Fourth, once the college decides to place emphasis and importance on general education, administrators need to ensure that the decision is publicized to encourage understanding across the campus. The administration should also be certain that it provides consistent information and detail to everyone, especially to administrators. Variations in information and understanding will only undermine any attempt to promote general education.

Fifth, administrators must take a leadership role in promoting and providing the necessary human and fiscal support to the established goals. It is not enough for administrators to say that they support general education, as they did in the CCGI (Cross and Fideler, 1989). They have the means to ensure that progress is made toward the college's goals. Provision of fiscal resources, personnel, and services to support the goal of making general education an important aspect of the college's education mission is a telling indication of clear, direct leadership. If there is not clear leadership from the president on down, the effort will not be perceived as serious and will fail. If the president and the deans, on the other hand, not only indicate on surveys that general education is a primary focus of their institution but also support their claims with public words and fiscal and temporal support and empower people at the college to emphasize general education, then there will be real success.

References

Center for the Study of Community Colleges. *An Analysis of Humanities Education in Two-Year Colleges: Phase 4.* Final report to the National Endowment for the Humanities. Los Angeles: Center for the Study of Community Colleges, 1978.

Center for the Study of Community Colleges. *Revitalizing the Humanities in the Community College: Final Report, October 1, 1979–September 30, 1982.* Los Angeles: Center for the Study of Community Colleges, 1982. 29 pp. (ED 230 250)

Cohen, A. M. *General Education and the Community College.* ERIC Digest. Los Angeles: ERIC Clearinghouse for Junior Colleges, 1988. 6 pp. (ED 304 196)

Cohen, A. M., and Brawer, F. B. *The Collegiate Function of Community Colleges: Fostering Higher Learning Through Curriculum and Student Transfer.* San Francisco: Jossey-Bass, 1987.

Cross, K. P., and Fideler, E. F. "Community College Missions: Priorities in the Mid-1980s." *Journal of Higher Education,* 1989, *60* (2), 209–216.

Raisman, N. A. "Moving into the Fifth Generation." *Community College Review,* 1990, *18* (2), 15–22.

NEAL A. RAISMAN *is associate provost and special assistant for university planning at the University of Cincinnati, Cincinnati, Ohio.*

Success in relation to general education tasks will occur in schools willing to modify institutional thinking to account for the part-time, nondegree nature of the student population, investment in student choice, and the community college approach to occupational education.

General Education in the Community College: Developing Habits of Thought

Judith S. Eaton

General education efforts are characterized by three distinct approaches. The first is the general education skills and ability approach: Emphasis is on the skills to be gained through a general education experience. This is essentially the strategy described by the Association of American Colleges (1988) Task Group on General Education. The second major approach is curriculum-bound: Specific courses or programs are required in order to maintain that students are generally educated. Some community colleges have utilized this strategy in building an interdisciplinary general education core curriculum for full-time, degree-seeking students. This approach also characterizes much of the thinking of the 1950s about general education (Johnson, 1982). The third approach identifies general education with distribution requirements for a degree in either a two-year or four-year setting. The requirements may be discipline-based or interdisciplinary, and they may be competence- or curriculum-based. Most important, the issue of a meaningful general education experience either in terms of skills to be developed, curricula to be studied, or distribution requirements to be filled is couched in language that assumes that students are seeking degrees, and that through the degree work the education experience is structured.

General education, including its status as a product of politics and other forces, its varying descriptions, and its position of significance in higher education, is a particularly challenging and even troublesome topic for the community college. This is not simply a matter of the community college's alleged disinterest in general education as a result of its multiple missions, its preoccupation with vocational education, or its local focus. There are three factors that make it especially difficult to establish effective general education programs at these two-year institutions, even at schools with the will and resources to ensure quality general education programs. These include the part-time, nondegree character of the student population, the community college attachment to the doctrine of student choice, and community college perception of its role in occupational education as precluding some traditional academic interests.

Current descriptions of general education applicable in a community college setting include Cohen and Brawer's (1987, p. 11) notion of general education as discipline-based courses designed to teach people to be enlightened citizens: "the conversion of the liberal arts into something practical." The Association of American Colleges (1988, p. 3) spoke of general education as "cultivation of the knowledge, skills, and attitudes that all of us use during most of our lives." Clark Kerr (1984, p. 33) described general education as "training in the basic skills and the provision of liberal learning opportunities." Boyer (1987) focused on the need for an integrated core, essential knowledge, connections across disciplines, and common experiences. Gaff (1988), summing up general education efforts in the 1980s, talked about the emphasis on content, coherence, and comprehensiveness as driving institutional attention to general education. Gaff (1989) later pointed out that we need to go beyond curriculum to consider whether or not the institutional culture supports general education.

General education has a mythic quality. Discussions about it are frequently dominated by the expectation that we will uncover an ideal vision of general education that will guide future academic decisions. We believe that we have a task of discovery as distinct from a task of development. A general education program should have a special status; we are not satisfied unless it reflects an academic ideal. Even while we are uncomfortable with the current state of our judgments about general education, we are reluctant to put forth additional descriptions or definitions because of our concern that they will be challenged and attacked. Either we want to be "right" about general education, or we do not wish to take any stand at all. We tend to approach general education decisions as if they can be made in ideal circumstances, unsullied by the usual politics accompanying many curriculum deliberations. This thinking is not realistic. General education programs are created and not discovered. The creation of general education programs involves not only intellectual considerations but serious and difficult political issues as well. The condition of general education at any given time is the result of political and intellectual pressure, compromise, and fashion as well as expression of academic values and preferences. General education preferences vary with time, politics, place, and academic interests. They also vary with the kind of institution, the nature of the faculty, and the kind of students served.

This chapter describes general education as an especially demanding challenge for community colleges. It discusses the difficulties in establishing viable general education programs in community colleges due to the part-time, nondegree nature of the community college student population, community college investment in student choice, and the community college approach to occupational education. It stresses that institutional success in relation to general education tasks will likely occur in those two-year schools willing to modify institutional thinking in these three areas. It urges that community colleges focus on general education as the development of certain habits of thought as a means of making general education viable in the community college setting. The increase in numbers of students not seeking a degree at both two-year and four-year institutions means that community colleges' success in meeting their general education challenge will provide important academic leadership for all of higher education.

General Education for Part-time, Nondegree Students

We can make sense of much of the advice in the literature on general education only if we assume that the realization of general education goals is dependent on degree-seeking students. General education expectations are set in the context of students persisting in a two-year or four-year degree program: Completion of the degree includes completion of general education requirements. Many of the recommendations to strengthen general education in community colleges (see, for example, Cohen and Brawer, 1989; Gaff, 1988; Johnson, 1982) assume that students, even if part-time, are seeking a degree and are responsive to the instructional directions that degree work carries.

The majority of two-year students, however, are enrolled part-time and are not degree seekers. There were more than 5.2 million students enrolled in community colleges in fall 1988 (Kroe, 1990). Data on degree and certificate acquisition in community colleges reveal that between 1976 and 1985, 400,000 to 456,000 students annually earned these credentials (Cohen and Brawer, 1989). The National Longitudinal Study of the High School Graduating Class of 1972 found that, after twelve years, approximately 24.5 percent of students earned an associate degree (Clifford Adelman, personal communication, May 17, 1990). This means that, in the community college, a major structure developed to set general education expectations, the degree structure, is irrelevant to large numbers of community college students.

If degrees are the vehicles by which community colleges design their attempts to realize their general education expectations, yet students do not get degrees, what do community colleges need to do if they wish to sustain general education? First, they must address the question of the student population for which they believe general education obligations are reasonable. Most community colleges want to be both flexible and responsible about student attendance and full- or part-time commitments. Many community colleges are comfortable separating the short-term or casual course takers from students who intend to earn a significant number of credits. Students who earn, for example, fewer than twelve credits may be exempt from any general education work. Those who enroll for twelve credits or more, on the other hand, would be held accountable for some general education work. This means that the colleges want to reasonably exclude some segment of the student population from any general education or other requirements and to reasonably include others. The issue then becomes one of determining how general education expectations can be attached to coursework or to programs that are of shorter duration than a two-year degree but require twelve or more credits.

There appear to be two ways in which general education can be incorporated at the course or short-program level. First, general education material can be integrated with specific course materials in either the liberal arts or the occupational education. Second, a core of general education work (for example, six or twelve credits) can be established in tandem with other community college work. Either of these approaches essentially fragments and minimizes the degree commitment to general education. These approaches also raise the question of whether the benefits of a general education experience, described in terms of curriculum undertaken or competencies gained, can be realized at the course or short-program level rather than the degree level. There are few examples of either approach to general education and little in the way of results to establish the effectiveness of either. The instructional directions for general education realized through coursework or shorter-than-degree programs have not been written.

The general education literature includes a number of desired goals. Institutions need to decide which goals to pursue and whether they need to develop yet other goals. Community colleges, for example, need to determine whether the model of incorporation of general education objectives in course material or the model of a general education core for shorter-than-degree programs can be used to realize the institutions' general education goals. The colleges need to develop other models as well. This calls for an institutional description of general education commitments. The colleges need to analyze the prevailing general education expectations such as coherence and connectedness to determine whether these expectations can be realized for nondegree students or whether some modification is needed.

Doctrine of Student Choice

There are a number of ways in which community colleges remain products of the 1960s. Their egalitarian commitment, the emphasis on breaking with tradition, the diminishment of the teacher as an authority, the increased importance of student decisions, the growing social role of the community college, and the dedication to women and minorities all describe this expanding sector of higher education. Community colleges were in many ways an experiment in being "other than" traditional collegiate education. This experiment included significant emphasis on student choice as manifested in the growing disregard for distribution requirements, the establishment of associate degrees with no requirements, and what some have called the cafeteria or market approach to the higher education experience. Students "did their own thing"—from protesting the Vietnam War, to civil rights marches, to choosing their courses and programs and deciding their degree directions.

The emphasis on student choice became embedded in community college thinking. Other than access, few other values in community college education are so strongly held or defended. Student choice was a measure of the extent to which the colleges were truly student-centered. Student choice was an indication of the extent to which community colleges respected their clientele. Student choice reflected the preferred "other than" position of community colleges in relation to traditional education. Student choice said that community colleges were not sites of traditional authoritarian behavior. The valuing of student choice manifested itself especially in the area of curriculum decisions. Counselors and faculty advisors sought to be supportive and nondirective, their tasks confined to assisting students in the making of curriculum decisions as distinct from directing students about what to do. Degree and other programs had a minimum of prerequisites and stipulations. Students could build a program at will. Many institutions offered degrees that suspended requirements entirely or allowed for generous substitution of one requirement for another in a degree program.

As the academic reform and assessment efforts, especially of the 1980s, placed an increasing number of demands on institutional effectiveness, community colleges were forced to reevaluate their commitment to student choice. Their renewed institutional commitment to general education in the form of requirements for courses, special programs, or degrees has proved incompatible with the thinking of the 1960s. The establishment of general education expectations or requirements calls for breaking with the doctrine of student choice. Insistence on general education requires community colleges to substitute, at least in part, institutional intervention for student decision making. At the most, community colleges can be flexible with general education requirements by providing a range of courses to meet general education goals. Increasingly, we find community colleges substituting institutional judgment in the form of degree requirements, prerequisites, and placement testing for primary reliance on student decision making. If handled in a sensitive and flexible manner, institutional intervention is an important and valuable dimension of student decision making. Whether as the result of renewed interest in general education or for other reasons, it is important that educators again provide direction and share judgments with students about their respective academic futures.

Occupational Education Role

There are three distinct forms of occupational education in community colleges. The first is the traditional degree program composed mainly of college-level courses with a concentration in a given career area such as nursing, accounting, or criminal justice. These offerings parallel what are called "professional" degree programs in four-year institutions and, increasingly, are articulated with them for transfer purposes. The second form of occupational education is the so-called terminal degree program, which is a credit program leading directly to employment without any particular emphasis on the potential of the program for further education, in particular, the baccalaureate experience. These programs were of particular importance to community colleges in the 1960s and 1970s when the paraprofessional job market was expanding dramatically and community colleges appeared to have found their appropriate niche within the higher education community. The third form of occupational education is the predominantly noncredit experience in the form of job training and retraining through short courses for occupational purposes. These courses are frequently offered at the request of business and industry in a local area.

In general, occupational or vocational educators in community colleges have had an ongoing concern that courses outside a particular career or vocational area were in some way in competition with intended vocational offerings. This concern included not only general education but also the liberal arts and even career coursework from other fields. General education, for example, has been viewed as a distraction from the primary technical training intent of such programs. It has been viewed as an obligatory but nonetheless annoying responsibility foisted on vocational educators. For those involved in short-term training programs, it is viewed as an essentially irrelevant, time-consuming drain on necessary study. Those responsible for the success of occupational education in community colleges feel that they have been saddled with outmoded notions of student performance that divert them from their fundamental responsibility: ensuring that their students function well in corporations, agencies, and organizations that require certain technical skills.

There are several issues here. First, general education skills *are* vocational skills; they are the generic competencies that we all need to be successful at virtually anything. I am referring here to effective reading and writing, basic knowledge of our society, and a fundamental understanding of the literature, art, and science that make up our worldview. We need these competencies. Second, the purposes of general education can be distinguished from the purposes of traditional discipline-based studies. General education does not purport to require the concentration of credits that, even at the community college level, would diminish the commitment to technical training. There should be room for general education in an occupational education curriculum. Third, we need to distinguish among the kinds of occupational education available in the community college. College-level transferable occupational education does not serve the same purpose as nontransferable ("terminal") credit occupational education, which does not serve the same purpose as short-term training. We have allowed the short-term training model and the narrowly focused vocational model to dominate our thinking about college-level career education. Thus, we believe that there is no room for general education in occupational education programs. Careful institutional differentiation among kinds of occupational education is needed with a resulting commitment to general education in those occupational efforts that can lead to further education.

Habits of Thought

Community colleges have two choices: They can change the students whom they serve to fit traditional general education expectations or they can tailor their approach to general education to the students whom they serve. In the first instance, community colleges can insist that students who matriculate into various liberal arts and occupational programs meet institutional degree requirements and thus be subject to general education determinations. They can enroll only students who are pursuing a degree. This approach would result in a shift in the degree-granting function of the community college from an incidental to a central activity of these institutions. It would, however, also likely result in diminished access to higher education for those students who cannot persist in an education program that has degree requirements. It probably would encourage some students to move to technical colleges without either general education or degree requirements. This, in turn, could result in fewer students pursuing the liberal arts and seeking a baccalaureate degree. The implications for access associated with community colleges that force a degree orientation on their students are so deleterious that community colleges are left to struggle with the problem of meeting general education expectations in light of the nondegree behavior of their clientele.

In the second instance, community colleges are confronted with the task of making changes in the manner in which they develop general education experiences to accommodate nondegree course-taking patterns of students. While structures to accomplish these objectives can be developed, they would raise serious intellectual questions about whether or not the results actually constitute general education. General education is frequently described as valuable because of the potential for assisting students with synthesis of information and ideas. It is more rather than less difficult to accomplish this synthesis through course taking as compared to sequential studies of some sort. Those who maintain that general education is characterized by curriculum coherence or connectedness would be skeptical that efforts to realize general education competence or curriculum goals can be successful in a course-taking mode. They would likely encourage community colleges to develop at least some sequential program structures short of a degree. They would further urge them not to rely on the course alone as the fundamental unit on which to establish general education expectations.

If general education effectiveness is considered a function of its comprehensiveness and coherence, what success can we expect to realize by attention to general education through isolated course-taking or shorter-than-degree programs? One way to approach this important academic difficulty is to envision general education as the establishment of certain habits of thought. General education would be less focused on curriculum issues and more concerned with helping students develop ways of approaching information and experience that strengthen their reasoning capacity, their awareness of relationships and responsibilities in a social and civic context, and their attention to values and moral issues. Coursework and program structures (short of a degree) can develop desired habits of thought derived from disciplinary and interdisciplinary study. Emphasis may be placed on strengthening the theoretical skills that enable students to be attentive to coherence and comprehensiveness issues in a variety of settings. General education pursued as the establishment of habits of thought does not require a degree orientation.

General education pursued as the cultivation of habits of thought involves attention to curriculum and pedagogy to ensure development of analytical and synthetic reasoning skills. Students in history courses, for example, would devote time to historical methodology as well as to historical narrative. They would be able to use the methods of thinking that produce historical inference in the study of history and elsewhere. Students in courses in mathematics would develop deductive and inductive reasoning skills that would be helpful in a variety of settings. The study of disciplines such as philosophy, psychology, or physics would call for students to become familiar with the forms of reasoning characteristic of these disciplines. Students who might pursue interdisciplinary coursework dealing with important moral and social issues would become adept at evaluating difficult and open-ended issues of societal values, norms, and beliefs.

To develop habits of thought, students first must expand their academic skills to incorporate modes of inference used in various disciplines or interdisciplinary work. Second, this expansion of academic skills results in the creation of an array of conceptual tools available and useful to students as they pursue education, a career, and life. Emphasis on the development of habits of thought is similar to the general education skills and ability approach in that the focus of curriculum and pedagogical efforts is the intellectual capacity gained through disciplinary and interdisciplinary study. The skills and ability approach emphasizes that students "identify perspectives, weigh evidence, and make wise decisions . . . to think about thinking and enjoy thinking" (Association of American Colleges, 1988, p.4). The skills and ability approach is intended for degree programs. Assistance to students to develop habits of thought does not require a degree setting.

This approach to general education can approximate some of the expectations of general education suggested by the descriptions offered above. It enables us to deal with the liberal arts as something practical. It meets the challenge of essential knowledge, the institutional culture supporting general education as well as providing knowledge, skills, and attitudes used during our lives. We can address habits of thought at a course, programmatic, departmental, or institutional level. We can develop expectations of student capacity in both occupational and academic areas and stress those capacities important to students whatever their education goals: education for work, baccalaureate education, or long-term personal interest education.

A focus on desired habits of thought as a means of meeting general education needs is consistent with efforts to modify past institutional emphasis on student choice and can assist in efforts to clarify the role of general education in occupational education. The institution can make decisions about general education requirements through courses and programs short of a degree. It can build general education expectations into course objectives. It can provide a basis for a minimum set of education experiences for all students who decide to persist at the community college. These requirements, expectations, and experiences can govern work both in the liberal arts and in occupational education. Community colleges, approaching general education as a responsibility to develop and strengthen habits of thought, will be in a position to serve their current student population, most of whom are non-degree-oriented, with greater effectiveness and responsiveness.

References

Association of American Colleges. *A New Vitality in General Education: Planning, Teaching, and Supporting Effective Liberal Learning by the Task Group on General Education.* Washington, D.C.: Association of American Colleges, 1988. 64 pp. (ED 290 387)

Boyer, E. L. *College: The Undergraduate Experience in America.* New York: Harper & Row, 1987.

Cohen, A. M., and Brawer, F. B. *The Collegiate Function of Community Colleges: Fostering Higher Learning Through Curriculum and Student Transfer.* San Francisco: Jossey-Bass, 1987.

Cohen, A. M., and Brawer, F. B. *The American Community College.* (2nd ed.) San Francisco: Jossey-Bass, 1989.

Gaff, J. G. "Reforming Undergraduate General Education." *Liberal Education,* 1988, 74 (5), 4–10.

Gaff, J. G. "General Education at Decade's End: The Need for a Second Wave of Reform." *Change,* 1989, 21 (4), 10–19.

Johnson, B. L. (ed.). *General Education in Two-Year Colleges.* New Directions for Community Colleges, no. 40. San Francisco: Jossey-Bass, 1982.

Kerr, C. "Liberal Learning: A Record of Presidential Neglect." *Change,* 1984, 16 (6), 32–36.

Kroe, E. *National Postsecondary Statistics, Collegiate and Noncollegiate: Fall 1989—Early Estimates, Survey Report.* Washington, D.C.: National Center for Education Statistics, 1990. 23 pp. (ED 317 122)

JUDITH S. EATON is president of the Council for Aid to Education in New York City. She was formerly vice president and director of the National Center for Academic Achievement and Transfer of the American Council on Education, Washington, D.C.

*Today's community college students need more than instruction in particular
disciplines as part of general education. They need to learn how to learn in
order to become expert self-regulated learners ready to enter into lifelong
learning.*

Broadening Our Conception of General Education: The Self-Regulated Learner

Claire E. Weinstein, Gretchen Van Mater Stone

When models of general education are derived from conceptions of expert
performance that focus entirely or primarily on knowledge enhancement,
they are doomed to failure (Carnevale, Gainer, Meltzer, and Holland, 1989;
Smith and Morris, 1989). This problem is particularly acute in relation to
the at-risk learner. Students who are at risk for academic failure or severe
underachievement may be either academically underprepared, indifferent
toward school success, or overextended in their school as well as out-of-
school commitments. These students need more than general knowledge
and basic competencies in computation, reading, and writing. Therefore,
educational models based only on transmission of knowledge, vocational
preparation, or both in the community college will not prepare students for
the lifelong learning so important to future growth and success. This con-
sideration is even more important for students who fall into the at-risk
category.

Expert-Novice Differences

Current studies investigating the nature of expert performance provide evidence for the complex nature of skilled functioning in both academic and
nonacademic contexts (Chi, Glaser, and Farr, 1988). For many years educators thought that an expert was simply someone who knew more about
something than most other people knew. These conceptions were really just
extensions of the Victorian idea of children as miniature adults. When children gained more (not different, just more) knowledge, skills, and social
graces, they would become adults. Now we know that there are both quan-

titative and qualitative differences between experts and novices (Alexander and Judy, 1988; Chi, Feltovich, and Glaser, 1981; Larkin, McDermott, Simon, and Simon, 1980; Lesgold, 1984; Means and Voss, 1985; Paris, Lipson, and Wixson, 1983).

In fact, there appear to be a number of major variables that differentiate experts and novices (Chi, Glaser, and Farr, 1988). The first, and the one that most individuals think is sufficient for expertise, is that experts know more (Chi, Glaser, and Rees, 1982; Means and Voss, 1985). The second, which may even be more important than the first, is that experts' knowledge is better organized and more integrated (Gobbo and Chi, 1986; Larkin, 1985; Larkin, McDermott, Simon, and Simon, 1980). The third is that experts have more effective and more efficient strategies for accessing and using their knowledge (Ericsson and Polson, 1988; Lesgold, 1984). The fourth is that experts seem to have different motivations for acquiring and using their knowledge (McCombs, 1989; Posner, 1988). And, finally, the fifth is that experts evidence more self-regulation in both the acquisition and application of their expertise (Chi, Glaser, and Farr, 1988). So, experts know more, their knowledge is better organized and integrated, they have better strategies and methods for getting to their knowledge, using it, applying it, and integrating it, and they have different motivations. Moreover, they tend to do these things in a more self-regulated manner. What are the implications of these findings for educational settings? What does it mean to be an expert learner?

What Does It Mean to Be an Expert Learner?

Types of Knowledge. Expert learners have a variety of different types of knowledge that can be classified into four basic categories. The first category is *knowledge about themselves as learners*. What are their preferences? What are their strengths? What are their weaknesses? What is the best time of day for them, the worst time? What are their interests and talents? What do they know about study habits, and what are their current study habits and practices? Knowledge about oneself as a learner in the context of postsecondary education helps one to orchestrate the resources needed to accomplish the studying and learning activities necessary for academic success. It is important to note that management of resources refers not only to external resources such as how often a learner sees a tutor or the amount of reading that the learner must do but also to how the learner orchestrates personal resources such as cognitive strategies, emotions, feelings, and study habits.

The second kind of knowledge that expert learners need is *knowledge about tasks*. If students do not know what is required to accomplish different kinds of educational tasks, different kinds of instructional tasks, and different kinds of evaluation tasks, then how will they know whether or not they have succeeded? For example, many students do not even understand how to read a textbook. They often treat every line as if it were just as important as every other line. Just think about how impossible a task it would be to read most college textbooks or manuals as if every line were just as important as every other line. Selecting out main ideas, knowing how to read for gist, knowing which facts are most important to recall—these are all part of being an expert reader who understands the task of reading college textbooks. Other types of academic tasks include listening, note taking, managing anxiety, writing papers, preparing for examinations, taking examinations, giving oral presentations, and dealing with procrastination.

The third type of knowledge needed by students to become expert learners is *knowledge about a wide variety of strategies, tactics, and study skills*. Students need a repertoire of learning approaches, strategies, and methods that they can use and adapt to a variety of academic as well as everyday learning situations. There are two major reasons that faculty and staff need to help students develop their own repertoires of studying and learning strategies. First, learners need to know about a variety of strategies and methods for learning before they can make mindful decisions about their preferences or the methods that seem to be most effective for them. Second, when students encounter academic difficulties, it is important for them to have a set of tools that they can use to resolve the problems.

The fourth area of knowledge necessary for the development of learning expertise is *knowledge about content*, often referred to as prior knowledge. It is easier for individuals to learn something new about a subject when they already know something about it. Part of the reason for this is that we already have an existing knowledge base that we can use to help us acquire the new information, to help us understand it, and to help us integrate it.

It is important to note that these four different types of knowledge interact. For example, students' knowledge about themselves as learners helps them to identify task characteristics that may be particularly problematic for them. Identification of these potential problems helps them to think about the learning strategies that they know might help them address these particular problems. When students can think about what they have already studied in an area, it may help them to create more meaning for the new material so that they can successfully complete the task and so on.

Comprehension Monitoring. Thus far, the discussion has focused on the four types of knowledge necessary to be an expert learner. However, these different types of knowledge are not sufficient for expertise. Expert learners must also know how to monitor their own comprehension. They need to know how to use self-assessment or self-testing to determine whether they are meeting their learning goals. There are many forms of self-assessment. It can be as simple as paraphrasing while reading or as complex as trying to teach new information or skills to someone else. Other forms of monitoring include trying to apply new knowledge, transforming it into another form such as a diagram or outline, and summarizing it. Each of these activities is designed to help students see if they really understand what they are studying and learning. Often, students believe that they understand but they do not test themselves to confirm or deny this belief. When they are wrong, that is, when they have only the "illusion of knowing," students think that they have reached their achievement goals and do not realize that they have not.

An expert learner can also generate fix-up strategies when problems arise. Fix-up strategies are the approaches and methods that students use to help remedy a learning problem. These methods can range from very simple activities such as rereading a confusing text section, to trying to reason through a problem-solving method, to going to a tutor for help, to learning with someone else who is taking the same course in order to study difficult sections together. Each of these activities is designed to help solve a learning problem. It is important that students have a repertoire of fix-up strategies so that they can deal with a variety of academic problems that might occur.

Thus far, the discussion has focused on a number of cognitive activities and control strategies that are necessary for expert learning. However, knowing *what* to do is not sufficient for effective learning. Knowing *how* to do it is still not sufficient for effective learning. Even knowing *when* to do it is not sufficient for effective learning. A student must also *want* to learn. Effective learning requires skill and will (Paris, Lipson, and Wixson, 1983; Zimmerman and Schunk, 1989).

Motivation. Current conceptions of self-regulated learning consider motivation to be a result of things we do or think, and things we do not do or think. Motivation has many components and interacts with and results from many factors. These factors include things such as the establishment and use of goals. It is not enough for students to have goals, they must also know how to use them to help generate and maintain the thoughts and actions necessary to achieve their goals. Another variable that affects motivation is efficacy expectations. This is the degree to which students believe that they can accomplish a task. If students do not believe that they can accomplish the task, then why try? If students do not have a strong sense that they can succeed at the tasks that they are being asked to perform in a community college setting, then why should they even try? This can be a particularly thorny and self-sabotaging problem for underprepared or at-risk students.

Motivation is also related to attributions, or where individuals place causality. To what do students attribute their successes? To what do they attribute their failures? If students do not attribute what happens to them in academic situations at least in part to their own efforts and abilities, rather than to the system, the teacher, or the difficulty of the test, why would they ever try again? Students must have a sense of empowerment to believe that their efforts will make a difference.

Finally, motivation is related to a number of other variables such as interest, valuing, and instrumentality. Thus, it is not a unidimensional factor. This has many implications for what needs to be done to increase and maintain student motivation.

Executive Control. Are the components of skill and will sufficient for expert learning? The answer is no. Another component is required. This component describes the means by which learners orchestrate and manage their own studying and learning. An expert learner is a self-regulated learner. Self-regulated learning requires skill, it requires will, and it requires executive control (Weinstein, 1988; Zimmerman, 1986; Zimmerman and Schunk, 1989).

Executive control refers to the processes whereby students orchestrate and manage their learning. This level of control involves a number of interacting activities. These steps are presented in a linear fashion, although in reality they interact and dynamically impact each other. The first step is *creating a plan*. How are students going to go about the study activity, whether it is preparing for a semester test, working on a project or paper, or reading a text? The next step is *selecting the specific strategies or methods* that they will use to achieve their goals. The third step is *implementing the methods* selected to carry out the plan. During the fourth step, students who are exercising control *monitor and evaluate* their progress on both a formative and a summative basis. Students who are self-regulating keep track of what they are doing and of how successful they are not only while they are implementing their plans but also at the end to see what they have accomplished. If students are not reaching their formative or summative goals, then they must modify what they are doing. This fifth step, *modifying, if necessary,* can involve any of the other components such as the plan, the methods, or even the original goal. Finally, students need to make an *overall evaluation* of what they have done and decide if the current approach would be an effective way to go about meeting similar goals in the future. This entire process helps students to build up a repertoire of strategies that they can call on in the future when a similar situation arises.

Now we have identified the major factors that generate and impact expertise in learning. An expert learner has skill, will, and a systematic approach to studying and learning. What are some of the implications of this conceptualization for community college instruction?

Implications for Instruction

There are strong instructional implications that can be derived from what is known about the characteristics of an expert learner. All three major components—skill, will, and executive control—involve cognitive processes. Cognitive processes require guided practice and feedback for their acquisition. The development of cognitive processes is also facilitated by modeling in a variety of contexts. In addition, transfer of strategies and approaches must be directly supported. One of the most significant findings in cognitive psychology is the degree to which cognitive strategies do not spontaneously transfer (Gick and Holyoak, 1980). Transfer can be enhanced by a number of methods, including direct instruction, varied practice, changing contexts, and use of a generalizable model, which people can refer back to and adapt to different situations.

Given what we know about the components of learning expertise and about how we can facilitate the development and elaboration of cognitive processes, what is the most effective way to teach students how to be effective learners? There are two basic approaches that have been used with some success to teach learning-to-learn strategies and skills. The first is called *direct instruction,* or the adjunct approach, where the instruction is supplementary to the usual curriculum. Something special is set up to focus specifically on learning how to learn as an adjunct to the standard courses that students take. It can range from a two-hour workshop taught by academic support personnel, to a two-week short course, to a semester-long course. A good example is a semester-long course offered in the Department of Educational Psychology at the University of Texas as part of the Cognitive Learning Strategies Project.

The formal title of this course is EDP310, Introduction to Educational Psychology: Individual Learning Skills. It is an academic course taken for fourteen weeks for a grade. There are approximately twelve hundred students per year in classes of twenty-eight taught by doctoral students from the Department of Educational Psychology, who also contribute greatly to course development activities. Instructors use a wide variety of content materials and instructional methods because the strategies and skills that are taught are useful in a variety of courses. Like any learning method, however, they must be applied in specific content areas to be learned. If we have a strategy that generalizes to more than one content area, then it is more generic, such as a strategy that applies to reading comprehension. If we have a strategy that is specific to one content area, then it is more content-dependent, such as a strategy for adding together two single-digit numbers. However, to learn a generic strategy, a student must have experience with it in a variety of content domains. This experience helps the student to learn the range of applicability of that particular strategy.

There are three groups of students who take this course. The first group is composed of students who are predicted to be at risk for failure at their time of entry into the University of Texas. Some of these students enter the university through special admissions programs, whereas others are identified through either admissions or diagnostic tests. Whatever the means of selection, they have been identified as having the same characteristics as students who have not succeeded in the past. The second group is composed of students who enter the university under the regular admissions procedures but then experience academic difficulties after they are enrolled. The third group includes students who are not experiencing academic difficulty, but who want to enhance their learning and study strategies repertoire. These three types of students are also found in the community college.

It is noteworthy that some of the difficulties often encountered by at-risk students relate to the differences between the academic contexts and demands of high school and those of college environments. The American high school is a highly teacher-directed environment. Typically, when a student experiences academic difficulty, the teacher recognizes that the student is having a problem, determines what the problem is, and then implements or guides the student to a solution. The difficulty with this system is that although students are learning the content in this situation, they are not learning how to monitor their own comprehension or how to remedy a similar academic problem should it arise again. Now, these students come to the university and they are sitting in a huge first year class. The odds are that the teacher cannot even see them, much less figure out if they are understanding what is being said. So our students must take more responsibility for their own learning in an environment for which they may or may not be prepared.

The students who take EDP310 tend to increase their grades by one grade point on a 4-point scale, tend to have a higher rate of retention at the university, and report greater satisfaction with the university as well as increases in self-esteem. However, these effects can be magnified by adding the second approach to teaching learning-to-learn strategies and skills—the *metacurriculum* approach.

Implementation of a metacurriculum involves embedding the teaching of learning-to-learn strategies and skills within content classes. Content area instructors and teaching assistants teach how to learn as well as what to learn. They try, for example, while they are teaching history, to help their students develop expertise as students of history. They try to teach students to become students of science as well as to learn about science. In fact, with students who are only somewhat deficient in their learning strategies and skills repertoire, this may be the method of choice since the aim is to hone their repertoire rather than to plug glaring holes in it.

For students with major learning-to-learn processing deficiencies, those at high risk for academic failure, a combination of the adjunct and the metacurriculum approaches is needed. In this combined approach, the adjunct programs focus on basic knowledge and fundamental mechanics for the different types of strategies and skills needed for self-regulated learning. The metacurriculum approach helps to provide varied practice with feedback and modeling needed to develop executive control, a vital component of a systematic approach to studying and learning. Implementation of the metacurriculum, either by itself or in combination with the adjunct approach, requires that faculty, teaching staff, and academic support personnel know how to combine the teaching of learning strategies with their normal instructional responsibilities. This has direct implications for faculty and staff development.

Implications for Assessment

In order to focus on the development of self-regulated learners, we must broaden our conceptions of entry-level student assessment. In addition to measures of reading ability, writing skills, and prior knowledge in mathematics or other content areas, we also need to assess students' learning and thinking strategies and skills. For example, the students who register for the learning skills and strategies course at the University of Texas complete a battery of tests that includes the Learning and Study Strategies Inventory (LASSI) (Weinstein, Palmer, and Schulte, 1987). The LASSI is a diagnostic and prescriptive instrument that helps students identify their learning and studying strengths and weaknesses so that they know where to concentrate their efforts to enhance their repertoire. The LASSI yields scores in ten different areas: attitude, motivation, time management, anxiety, concentration, information processing, selecting main ideas, study aids, self testing, and test strategies. Students are taught how to combine this information with the data from their other entry-level measures to set priorities for their work in the course.

Conclusion

In our rapidly changing world, educational models based on either knowledge transmission, vocational preparation, or both will not prepare students for lifelong learning, job enhancement, or career advancement. The future belongs to individuals who can identify their own learning needs and who have the resources needed to capitalize on their experiences to orchestrate and manage their own learning activities. Community colleges, as well as other postsecondary institutions, must broaden their definitions of general education to include the development of self-regulated learners.

References

Alexander, P. A., and Judy, J. E. "The Interaction of Domain-Specific and Strategic Knowledge in Academic Performance." *Review of Educational Research*, 1988, *58*, 375–404.

Carnevale, A. P., Gainer, L. J., Meltzer, A. S., and Holland, S. I. "Workplace Basics: The Skills Employers Want." *Community, Technical, and Junior College Journal*, 1989, *59* (4), 28–33.

Chi, M.T.H., Feltovich, P. J., and Glaser, R. "Categorization and Representation of Physics Knowledge by Experts and Novices." *Cognitive Science*, 1981, *5*, 121–152.

Chi, M.T.H., Glaser, R., and Farr, M. J. (eds.). *The Nature of Expertise*. Hillsdale, N.J.: Erlbaum, 1988.

Chi, M.T.H., Glaser, R., and Rees, E. "Expertise in Problem Solving." In R. Sternberg (ed.), *Advances in the Psychology of Human Intelligence*. Vol. 1. Hillsdale, N.J.: Erlbaum, 1982.

Ericsson, K. A., and Polson, P. G. "A Cognitive Analysis of Exceptional Memory for Restaurant Orders." In M.T.H. Chi, R. Glaser, and M. J. Farr (eds.), *The Nature of Expertise*. Hillsdale, N.J.: Erlbaum, 1988.

Gick, M. L., and Holyoak, K. J. "Analogical Problem Solving." *Cognitive Psychology*, 1980, *12* (3), 306–355.

Gobbo, C., and Chi, M.T.H. "How Knowledge Is Structured and Used by Expert and Novice Children." *Cognitive Development*, 1986, *1*, 227–237.

Larkin, J. H. "Understanding, Problem Representations, and Skill in Physics." In S. F. Chipman, J. W. Segal, and R. Glaser (eds.), *Thinking and Learning Skills*. Vol. 2: *Research and Open Questions*. Hillsdale, N.J.: Erlbaum, 1985.

Larkin, J. H., McDermott, J., Simon, D. P., and Simon, H. A. "Models of Competence in Solving Physics Problems." *Cognitive Science*, 1980, *4*, 317–345.

Lesgold, A. M. "Acquiring Expertise." In J. R. Anderson and S. M. Kosslyn (eds.), *Tutorials in Learning and Memory*. San Francisco: W. H. Freeman, 1984.

McCombs, B. "Self-Regulated Learning and Academic Achievement: A Phenomenological View." In B. J. Zimmerman and D. H. Schunk (eds.), *Self-Regulated Learning and Academic Achievement: Theory, Research and Practice*. New York: Springer-Verlag, 1989.

Means, M. L., and Voss, J. F. "Star Wars: A Developmental Study of Expert and Novice Knowledge Structures." *Journal of Memory and Language*, 1985, *24*, 746–757.

Paris, S. G., Lipson, M. Y., and Wixson, K. K. "Becoming a Strategic Reader." *Contemporary Educational Psychology*, 1983, *8*, (3), 293–316.

Posner, M. I. "Introduction: What Is It to Be an Expert?" In M.T.H. Chi, R., Glaser, and M. J. Farr (eds.), *The Nature of Expertise*. Hillsdale, N.J.: Erlbaum, 1988.

Smith, A., and Morris, D. "Presidential Perspectives on Teaching and Learning." *Community, Technical, and Junior College Journal*, 1989, *59* (5), 30–36.

Weinstein, C. E. "Executive Control Processes in Learning: Why Knowing How to Learn Is Not Enough." *Journal of College Reading and Learning*, 1988, *21*, 48–56.

Weinstein, C. E., Palmer, D. R., and Schulte, A. C. *Learning and Study Strategies Inventory*. Clearwater, Fla.: H & H, 1987.

Zimmerman, B. J. "Becoming a Self-Regulated Learner: Which Are the Key Subprocesses?" *Contemporary Educational Psychology*, 1986, *11* (4), 307–313.

Zimmerman, B. J., and Schunk, D. H. (eds.). *Self-Regulated Learning and Academic Achievement: Theory, Research, and Practice*. New York: Springer-Verlag, 1989.

Claire E. Weinstein is professor in the Department of Educational Psychology, University of Texas, Austin.

Gretchen Van Mater Stone is adjunct assistant professor in the Department of Educational Psychology, University of Texas, Austin.

Students acquire values from general education courses, with the values determined, at least partly, by the instructor's teaching methods. Four methods for teaching values are described in this chapter: direct indoctrination, rationalized indoctrination, delineated options, and student values clarification.

Teaching Values Through General Education

R. Murray Thomas

The issue at hand is not "Should values be taught in college classes?" Instead, the question is, "Since values are inevitably espoused in college classes, which values should be highlighted and by what means can they most effectively be conveyed?" The argument advanced in this chapter is that many general education courses fail to teach values nearly as effectively as they teach facts, concepts, theories, and processes, and that an analysis of the teaching of values can suggest steps that might be taken to improve the convictions that students acquire in their general education experience.

Nature of Values

At the outset, it is useful to distinguish values from facts, concepts, theories, and processes. Facts, as the term is used here, are descriptions of either (1) discrete observations and measurements of people, objects, or events or (2) summaries of such observations and measurements. Statements of fact tell what exists and in what amount. Examples of facts are the structure of a cattleya orchid, the population distribution in Japan, the Battle of Waterloo, and the invention of the transistor. Concepts represent qualities shared by a cluster of facts. A concept identifies a way in which several objects, people, or events are alike. Typical concepts encountered in college classes are electrons, chemical compounds, crustal plates, recessive genes, culture, social class, cost-benefit, and mezzo forte. Theories, broadly speaking, are proposals about which facts are most important to identify and how those facts are interrelated. Hence, a theory or a model is a scheme for organizing facts and concepts. In general education courses, students can encounter theories of

 41

relativity, the big bang, the evolution of languages, human motivation, neurotic behavior, social change, political organization, and much more. Processes are sets of procedures for accomplishing specifiable ends. Illustrations of processes include photosynthesis, using a microscope, painting a portrait, playing a violin, conducting a public opinion survey, planning a battle, operating a microcomputer, speaking a foreign language, and writing a short story.

Values, in contrast, are opinions about the desirability or propriety or goodness of something. The "something" may be objects, events, people's behavior, policies, processes, ideas, or the like. Statements about values tell whether something is good or bad, better or worse, well done or poorly done, suitable or unsuitable. Values are typically attached to certain of the facts, concepts, theories, and processes that are taught. For instance, one fact may be judged better than another because it is founded on more secure evidence. One concept is considered more useful than others because it encompasses more phenomena. One theory has better empirical support than another, and one process is deemed more efficient than its competitors. From my observation, general education courses are chiefly directed at teaching facts, concepts, theories, and processes. The teaching of values is usually given far less conscious attention, and improperly so.

Values by Types. One convenient way to analyze values is to divide them into eight types: aesthetic, moral, social-conventional, personal welfare, technical or functional, scientific, political, and economic. Inspection of these categories may suggest to an instructor which types he or she would like to include in a general education class. Aesthetic values concern artistic matters. Aesthetic values, when expressed about a painting, a poem, a drama, or a musical performance, are reflected in such phrases as "very precise in conveying the essence of the landscape," "nicely turned metaphors," "brutally realistic," and "in the highest classical tradition."

Moral values typically concern standards of social behavior, that is, standards of human relationships. The term *moral values* also refers to the relationship between people and supernatural beings, so that failure to abide by God's laws becomes a moral issue. And in some people's opinion, morality may extend as well to nonhuman aspects of nature—animals, plants, and such inanimate objects as lakes and mountains. Thus, not everyone agrees on what sorts of phenomena belong within the moral domain. For instance, Turiel (1980) has contended that writers often fail to distinguish between matters of morality and matters of social convention. From Turiel's viewpoint, moral issues relate solely to acts bearing on justice. These are acts that can cause physical or psychological harm to others, violate others' rights, and influence the general welfare. He proposes that, in contrast to moral standards, social conventions such as "conventional styles of dress, forms of greeting, and rules of games" (1980, p. 364) constitute shared knowledge of uniformities in social interactions and are determined by the social system in which they are formed. While moral and social-conventional values focus on the treatment of other people, personal welfare values are self-centered. They refer to "my welfare and my rights," "what I deserve," "what others owe me," and "what I owe myself."

Technical or functional values are concerned with how efficiently something operates or how well people perform their roles. The application of functional values is reflected in such phrases as "a user-friendly computer," "a badly run delivery service," and "a well-taught class." Scientific values pertain to how faithfully studies of the natural and social world adhere to the canons of scientific investigation. Judgments based on these canons result in such comments as "inadequate sampling of the population," "convincing replication of the earlier experiment," and "sloppy preparation of the microscope slides." Political values relate to the exercise of influence, power, and control over other people. Such values involve convictions about who has the right to be in charge, to give orders to others, to enjoy special privileges, and to determine the sanctions or rewards that should be meted out to people. Political values also serve as the bases for judgments about the methods by which people assume power over others and the methods they subsequently use to exert that power. Remarks reflecting political values include "unwarranted massive use of force," "fair election," "defamation of character," and "proper respect for individual rights." Economic values refer to the monetary worth of something and to how people perform as producers and consumers. Typical remarks centering on economic values are "wise investment," "disastrous negative cash flow," "rare bargain," "junk bonds," "smart shopper," and "fiscal irresponsibility."

It should be apparent that these eight types of values are not mutually exclusive but often overlap. Aesthetic values within a given society may represent social conventions, as in styles of dress and architecture, whereas political values frequently involve issues of morality, as in questions of honesty in public office and the exploitation of minority groups.

Values by Subject Matter Fields. General education classes are sometimes structured as cross-discipline courses bearing such titles as The Development of Civilization or Problems of Modern Living. In other cases, classes are organized under academic discipline or subject matter titles such as Contemporary Art, World Literature, Political Structures, Psychological Foundations, and Health Education. An instructor's task becomes one of deciding which kinds of values will be addressed in his or her course. Frequently, the value of a given item (with item referring to a fact, concept, theory, process, or other idea) is not considered in isolation but rather is judged in relation to one or more other items. Hence, democracy is compared with communism, Bach with the Beatles, Picasso with Andy Warhol, psychoanalysis with behaviorism, and a low-fat diet with a high-fat diet. The instructor's intention, either stated outright or merely implied, is to have students, when confronted by such pairings, prefer one of the options over the other, that is, make a value choice. The question in every case is, "What values are involved in considering one of the options to be superior to the other?" The assumption here is that instructors who include such topics in their classes believe either (1) that one of the pair is better than the other and that they should tell the students why and/or (2) that students should apply their own values in choosing between the alternatives and should be prepared to explain the nature of their values.

Choosing Methods for Teaching Values

Once an instructor has selected a topic to describe and appraise, the next step is to select a method for presenting the topic and for applying value judgments to it. Whereas the process of choosing the method of presenting the topic is clearly conscious and intentional, the method for attaching a value appraisal oftentimes is not. From my observations of college teaching over the past five decades, I have concluded that the teaching of values is too frequently unintentional, incidental, inefficient, and inadequately evaluated. By *unintentional* and *incidental* I mean that many of the values that students acquire in a class may not be directly planned by the instructor. For instance, values can be conveyed incidentally by the teacher's manner of commenting on a topic. Any remark that reflects the speaker's admiration and approval or dismay and disgust implies a value judgment: "Ralph Waldo Emerson called Poe 'the jingle man,' and that's all Poe was, just a clever rhymer"; "El Greco painted human figures, he elongated them in a weird way"; "Teddy Roosevelt had the right idea—walk softly and carry a big stick"; "Supply-side economics would work if Congress would just give the plan a chance"; "The government has no business requiring drug or AIDS testing."

In a similar way, teachers' values can be implied by their reactions to students' questions or comments, whether the reaction is agreement, derision, or disbelief: "You're right. Debussy was more inventive than Franz Lehar"; "Where did you ever get the idea that humanistic theory made better sense than behaviorism?"

Sometimes, a teacher's mode of response belies the content of his or her remarks, so that the value that is verbally advocated is not reflected in the teacher's manner when reacting to student comments. In such cases, students may learn more about values from the teacher's mode than from the described value. Such is the case when an instructor uses sarcasm as a device to control argumentative class members.

Intentional Teaching of Values

It seems clear that if the values that students acquire are those that the instructors truly want to convey, then it is best for instructors to intentionally build the value judgment aspect of their lessons into their teaching methods. There are several ways of approaching this task, with each way implying a somewhat different instructional goal. The following examples depict four methods for teaching values: direct indoctrination, rationalized indoctrination, delineated options, and student values clarification. Teaching involves direct indoctrination when the instructor not only explains an idea or event or process but also assesses its worth. The instructor's goal in such instances is to have the students accept an evaluation as correct without a precise explanation of the criteria on which the judgment was founded. And while the term *indoctrination* is used here to label a teaching approach, the term is not necessarily to be interpreted in a pejorative sense. Rather, it simply means that a single point of view is espoused by the instructor: "That's the proper way to solve such an equation"; "Assassinating the tyrant was the only sensible solution"; "It's amazing that they included any of Leigh Hunt's work in an anthology, since his verses were so insignificant."

Rationalized indoctrination consists of the teacher's application of a value judgment to the topic, and then a description of the line of logic that led to the judgment. The aim here is to have students accept the instructor's opinion as valid and to understand the values on which the judgment was founded: "The survey was flawed by the researchers sampling only 685 college students in New York, then drawing conclusions about the sex behavior of American college students in general"; "As a poetic form, the sonnet is superior to free verse because the sonnet's precise meter and rhyme scheme demand far greater ingenuity on the part of the poet than does free verse"; "Reducing the tax rate on capital gains will help the rich but hurt the general population by shifting the tax burden onto wage earners and retired people who don't have big investments."

In the delineated options approach, the instructor describes more than one alternative for how the matter being discussed could be evaluated and then tells which values underlie each alternative. The instructor's intention is to show how different value considerations can lead to different appraisals of the matter at hand, whether or not the instructor divulges his or her own preference: "Not everyone views social welfare provisions in the same way. For example, Democrats traditionally have advocated the government providing a wide range of social services as a way to eradicate poverty, while Republicans have proposed that too much government welfare breeds dependence and discourages self-reliance" (no expressed preference); "In accounting for markedly deviant behavior, biologists are apt to look for the cause in genetics and body chemistry, whereas sociologists more often seek causes in the person's social environment. I believe there's a lot more to genetic and body chemistry causes than most people think. But, of course, I'm a biologist" (an expressed preference).

The term *values clarification* is used here to refer to a teaching method in which an instructor, first, describes a variety of values that might be applied in judging the issue under discussion. Then the instructor requires the students to express their own judgments and explain the values on which such judgments are founded. The purpose of this approach is to furnish students practice in (1) identifying types of values that can be applied in appraising the topic at hand, (2) weighing the desirability of the various values in terms of the students' own philosophies of life, (3) making their own appraisals of the topic, and (4) defending their appraisals in terms of a rationale (explanations of why they prefer certain values over others, and how these preferences have logically led to their judgments on the topic). Such a process can result in different students coming up with different judgments as a result of the particular values that they apply to the topic. The following examples represent two students' decisions about the treatment of people found guilty of drunk driving: "Drunk driving is a very serious offense. But we have to recognize that most people do drink alcohol, so it's not unusual for people who are quite good citizens to make the mistake of driving after they've had a couple of drinks. Therefore, on their first or even second offense, they should only be put on probation, just as a warning, whether or not their driving led to an accident. I believe in compassion. People deserve a second or third chance. It's in keeping with the spirit of 'Peace on earth, good will to all men'"; "At least half of the traffic deaths each year involve drunk drivers. Drunk driving is so socially destructive that strict measures must be taken to get these people off the streets. Anyone caught driving while drunk should go to jail for at least three months and have driving privileges revoked for at least three years. I believe in 'Peace on earth to men of good will.' But people who drink and drive are socially irresponsible, self-indulgent, and not of good will. Serious irresponsibility deserves serious punishment."

Adjusting an Instructional Approach to the Occasion

Of course, instructors may adapt one of the above approaches on one occasion and a different approach on another, depending on the circumstances that mark the two occasions. By *circumstances* I mean such conditions as (1) the controversiality of the topic of discussion, (2) its social significance, and (3) the time and space available to discuss the topic.

Some topics studied in general education classes are more controversial than others, in the sense that there is greater disagreement in society about the desirability of some events or policies than of others. For example, more people agree on the desirability of preventing heart attacks than on the desirability of abortion. As a consequence, an instructor can decide that it is important to use a delineated options or a values clarification approach with the abortion issue, but either a direct or a rationalized indoctrination when discussing heart attack prevention. The rationale behind such a decision is that highly controversial matters such as abortion need to be analyzed in detail so that students can understand the complex values arguments adduced to support each side of the issue. In contrast, the values undergirding people's attitudes toward noncontroversial topics such as the prevention of heart attacks are usually so obvious that they do not warrant detailed inspection.

Some topics also have greater social consequences than others. Social consequences refers to how seriously a topic affects people's lives and to how many people are affected. In recent history, the Vietnam War had greater social consequences than the fifty-five-miles-an-hour speed limit on public highways. Therefore, an instructor might choose to use a student values clarification approach with the Vietnam War but only a delineated options approach with the speed limit topic. The amount of class time, of homework time, and of reading materials space (textbooks, library reading assignments, and so on) that instructors believe a given topic deserves can also influence which way they address values related to the topic. A prominent example of such time and space constraints is the treatment given in biology courses to theories about the origin of the human species. Advocates of the biblical interpretation of human origins have lobbied state legislatures to require that the time and space in biology classes dedicated to the question of human beginnings be divided equally between the creationist view and the Darwinian view. However, the great majority of the nation's biology instructors have opposed such a plan, giving as their reasons that the objective evidence in support of a Darwinian position is far greater than that supporting the creationist position and that the time and space needed to analyze both positions thoroughly is so great that other important topics in the course would have to be eliminated. Therefore, they have chosen to present in detail only the theory that they consider the more convincing— Darwin's view—and to make little or no mention of the competing theory. In effect, they consider creationism not worth the time and space available for discussion. As a consequence, they typically use rationalized indoctrination in teaching about human beginnings.

Importance of Stated Criteria

When instructors lecture or students engage in discussions, one of the greatest weaknesses in their presentations is their failure to specify the criteria that undergird their value judgments. One of the most common causes of this failure is the speakers' lack of clarity about the substance of their own values criteria. They say, "I disagree with his policy" or "that picture is the best of the lot" or "I don't find that argument very convincing," without identifying the exact reasons for their judgments. When asked to explain further, they may need to ponder what sort of values are behind their intuitive judgments. However, sometimes those who are asked to explain their choices continue to be at a loss in identifying the specific values on which their opinions rest, so they persist in responding with vague reasons: "That's the way it seems to me" or "I have a feeling about it" or "It's just the way I look at it." In these cases, an instructor or classmate may help them discover the nature of their values by means of a process of probing. The technique involves exploration of the individual's preference among two or more options, then comparison of the options' likenesses and differences in order to locate the specific values that led that person to choose one alternative over another. The following simulated conversation between an instructor and student in a world literature course demonstrates one way of conducting a probe intended to foster student values clarification:

STUDENT: The play *Our Town* is really better than *Death of a Salesman.*

INSTRUCTOR: In what way? Exactly what makes it better?

STUDENT: Well . . . there's more to it.

INSTRUCTOR: Sorry, but I don't understand. More what?

STUDENT: Oh . . . I'd say it's more upbeat.

INSTRUCTOR: You mean more optimistic? Happy ending? Remember, key characters in both plays die. Death's an important issue in both of them.

STUDENT: Well . . . yeah. Not exactly a happy ending, of course. But *Our Town* made me think of something important that I should be doing in my life. It's that we ought to treasure each day, pay attention to love, to little things we tend to take for granted.

INSTRUCTOR: And you didn't get that kind of message from *Death of a Salesman?*

STUDENT: Oh, I suppose it might have a little of that in it, but really not much. The point of *Death of a Salesman* was different. It's a good play, but not up to *Our Town.*

INSTRUCTOR: So you think a play is better if it teaches you something about how to make your life better, about how to enjoy your own life? Is that it?

STUDENT: Not exactly "enjoy," but more like appreciate . . . be grateful. But I suppose that's a kind of enjoyment.

INSTRUCTOR: If I'm not mistaken, you've just now specified a value you use in preferring one play over another?

STUDENT: (Ponders again.) Now this is just my own personal opinion, but I like them both. I wouldn't put one over the other. *Our Town* is a lot simpler to understand, since it's in everyday modern language.

INSTRUCTOR: That means ease of understanding is one of the values you apply?

STUDENT: Yes, I think so. But still, there are some really great lines in *Hamlet.* That speech about "to be or not to be" and then Polonius's advice to his son who was going off to England. Some great ideas there.

INSTRUCTOR: Why were they great ideas?

STUDENT: They tell some important things about life. And Shakespeare said them so well . . . the words he picked and the rhythm of the lines.

INSTRUCTOR: All right. Now let's go back and see what you've come up with. I asked you why you preferred one play over another. Now you've explained some of the specific values you use in judging literature. See if I have them right. You value works that teach important truths about life, particularly truths that help you appreciate and make the most of your own daily life. Also, you value works that are easy to understand, but you're willing to struggle with the wording if the truths are cast in language that is particularly enlightening and rhythmic—pleasing to the ear. Is that correct?

STUDENT: That's about it.

As the above dialogue demonstrates, the instructor's purpose has been to aid the student in raising values criteria from a subconscious, intuitive level to a conscious level where they can be described, examined, and explained to other people. It may be apparent that this process of rationalizing subliminal values is easier and more successful in subject matter fields that depend on the cognitive manipulation of verbal and mathematical symbols. It is less successful in the arts, where the media are nonverbal and nonmathematical. However, even for such areas as the arts and physical activities, the sort of probing illustrated above is a worthwhile exercise in helping students identify the beliefs that underlie their value judgments.

Assessing Students' Acquisition of Values

If one of the objectives of a general education course is to teach values—or even if values are incidentally conveyed to students—then it seems important to determine which values students have acquired from the course. This brings us to the question of how values assessment can reasonably be conducted. The answer differs according to the values instruction approach used in the course—direct indoctrination, rationalized indoctrination, delineated options, or student values clarification. It seems likely that an instructor who engages in direct indoctrination will want to discover how well students understand and remember the value positions that he or she advocated. An assessment device for accomplishing this could be a multiple-choice test introduced by the following directions: "For each of the multiple-choice items below, mark with an X the choice that best matches the point of view advocated by the instructor of this course." An instructor who practices rationalized indoctrination will want to know not only how well students grasped the position that he or she expressed but also whether they can describe the values or line of logic supporting that position. Again, a multiple-choice test could serve such a purpose if it includes directions such as the following: "For each of the multiple-choice items below, mark with an X the choice that best matches the point of view advocated by the instructor of this course. Then, on the line beneath the item, tell what values belief is reflected in that point of view."

Assessment from the perspective of a delineated options instructor might consist of either multiple-choice or matching items introduced with these directions: "Under each of the following items you find two statements, A and B, expressing different attitudes toward a person, product, theory, or policy. Below each statement you find a list of values. Your task is to indicate which of these values logically support statement A and which support statement B. Indicate your decisions by writing the letter A on the line in front of each value appropriate to statement A and letter B on the line in front of each value appropriate to statement B."

In the case of a student values clarification approach, the assessment can require class members both to describe their own judgments of an issue and to support these judgments with lines of logic that include descriptions of the values on which their judgments have been founded. The directions could be the following: "In the case of each of the statements below, first, tell whether you agree or disagree with the position expressed in the statement and then describe the values you would offer in support of your decision."

As a final issue, there is the question of how students' answers to the foregoing types of test items should be assessed and graded. In cases of direct indoctrination, rationalized indoctrination, and delineated options, the method is simple. The instructor merely judges how closely students' answers match the values that the instructor endorsed in the course. The closer the match, the higher the students' grades. But in a true student values clarification approach, the criterion cannot be how closely the students' opinions matched the instructor's, since students are expected to choose and defend their own value judgments, whether or not these judgments correspond to the instructor's convictions. Hence, students' answers should be judged against standards different from agreement with the instructor's values, that is, on such criteria as how lucidly students explain their values, the internal consistency of their arguments, and how well their answers cover the facets of the issue at hand.

Conclusion

The purpose of this chapter has been to describe types of values often found in general education courses and to illustrate four approaches to teaching values and to assessing how well students achieve the goals of each approach. It is my conviction that in many general education classes, students would profit significantly if instructors gave greater attention to teaching values and to assessing the outcomes.

Reference

Turiel, E. "The Development of Social-Conventional and Moral Concepts." In M. Windmiller, N. Lambert, and E. Turiel (eds.), *Moral Development and Socialization*. Boston: Allyn & Bacon, 1980.

R. MURRAY THOMAS *is professor emeritus in the Graduate School of Education, University of California, Santa Barbara.*

*For general education to succeed in providing the knowledge and under-
standing that students need now and will need in the future, it must provide
a basis for global understanding and thinking. Practical approaches to
achieve this goal are suggested.*

Globalizing General Education: Changing World, Changing Needs

Douglas P. Sjoquist

At no other time in human history have we been more acutely aware of the
changing character of the world in which we live, and this rapid change is
forcing us to recast the nature and scope of the general education curriculum. Throughout this decade, higher education will focus on the question
of what kinds of literacies will enable our students to meet the challenges
of living and working in what Alvin Toffler (1970) calls the Third Wave
civilization. Whether or not we embrace the model that Toffler uses in ex-
plaining human history (that is, in terms of scientific and technological
waves of change), we will have to respond to the changing needs of our
students if we are going to help them (and ourselves) prepare for and
thrive in the future.

While no one would deny that a general education curriculum should
contain courses designed to improve the proficiencies of our students in
basic subject areas such as mathematics, writing, and the natural and social
sciences, we would be arrogant and grossly negligent in our commitment
to general education if our only aim was functional literacy. Another goal
must be the acquisition of basic concepts and principles related to the
world community. Courses that promote an understanding of the cultural
and geographical relationships among the peoples who constitute our planetary civilization and contribute to the interdependence—ecological, political, economic, and so on—of our world are particularly germane to the
general education curriculum as we move through the 1990s toward the
next century.

Expanding the Concept of Cultural Literacy

Although cultural literacy has become apropos to the general education curriculum, it should not be defined within the narrow framework of Western civilization. Can Americans afford to be culturally myopic in a world that has become increasingly interdependent politically, economically, and environmentally? The task of improving the abilities of our students to understand the nature and dynamics of our contemporary "global village" requires that we adopt a globalized concept of cultural literacy. This is not to argue that faculty (and our students) must become specialists in and intimately familiar with a seemingly infinite mass of fact-oriented information related to the history of world civilizations. Given the rapidly changing character of our world, it is doubtful that any single list of factual information, for example, the five thousand or so terms that Hirsch (1988) recommends for cultural literacy, would remain useful throughout one's lifetime. Also, we cannot assume that knowing a list of terms makes an individual literate.

What is vital to our students is some degree of knowledge and understanding of the priorities and values of not only our own culture but other cultures as well. A general education curriculum needs to place emphasis on the acquisition of concepts and attitudes that enable students to creatively, intelligently, and compassionately respond to change and diversity. Globalization of our approach to cultural literacy can do no less than increase the students' possibilities for cultural enrichment, help them cultivate a concept of civilization as it relates to the full range of human experience, and foster a greater awareness of and sensitivity to the interdependence of our planet's peoples and systems.

Questions Concerning a
Western-Grounded Curriculum

The National Endowment for the Humanities (NEH) report *50 Hours: A Core Curriculum for College Students* (Cheney, 1989) recommended that beginning college students take up the study of Western and American civilizations before studying African, Asian, or pre-Columbian American cultures. The rationale for that approach was that Western American culture is readily accessible and that "diverse traditions are best approached by students who are first grounded in one" (Cheney, 1989, p. 25). Specifically, the report recommended that students be required to take in sequence an origins of civilization course and a Western civilization course in their freshman year, and a second Western civilization course and an American civilization course as sophomores. Should the core courses for the community college student, who may or may not transfer to a four-year institution, be restricted to Western and American civilizations?

Obviously, if the NEH approach were adopted and implemented at the community college level, it would be possible for students to terminate their academic studies after two years to attend college without ever having been exposed to the worldviews of three-fourths of the world's population! This prospect is especially disturbing when one considers that the likelihood of our students eventually working for a company that does international business is much greater today than in the past. Only those students transferring to a four-year college or university would be required (in their junior and senior years) to study a non-Western cultural tradition and thereby be given an opportunity to develop an expanded vision of the world. Must a student attend a four-year institution to be given the opportunity to acquire knowledge necessary in the world?

One of the questionable assumptions underlying the NEH approach is that the study of Western civilization provides students with an occasion to discover their cultural roots. What we often choose to ignore, however, is that our student body is not culturally homogeneous. This is particularly true at urban community colleges. Included in our classrooms are students who come from a wide range of ethnic and cultural backgrounds. Furthermore, minority student enrollments at the community college level are increasing in many regions of the United States. Minority enrollments increased by about 21 percent from fall 1980 to fall 1987. In fall 1987, approximately 22 percent of all students enrolled in two-year colleges were minorities. By the year 2000, minority enrollment will constitute an even greater percentage of the total student enrollment at two-year institutions (El-Khawas, Carter, and Ottinger, 1988). It could be argued that we are depriving many of our students of a chance to discover their cultural heritages by limiting our teaching to Western civilization and culture.

Another dubious assumption of the plan to have students first study the Western tradition before taking classes that deal with other world civilizations is that our cultural roots are uniquely European. This is simply not true. Many non-Western civilizations have made notable linguistic, religious, artistic, political, scientific, and technological contributions to the so-called Western tradition. Although we tend to disregard it, the growth and development of Western civilization has been shaped to a significant degree by cultural influences emanating from African and Asian sources. Our cultural roots extend into the global community and are not exclusively European!

The plan to have students pursue the examination of Western and American civilizations first because these are readily accessible is seemingly pragmatic, but, on the other hand, it may reflect our inability (or unwillingness) to see the influences and elements of other world cultures in our own cultural tradition or even in our own community. Clearly, the U.S. population is multicultural, and revolutions in communications and transportation have made the world readily accessible. We are also inclined to support the notion that students are better prepared to investigate and understand "diverse traditions" when the students are first anchored in their own tradition.

However, what is to prevent students from seeing only that which is Western? What is to prevent them from measuring the beliefs, values, and accomplishments of other cultural traditions by Western standards? While such an approach may better enable students to distinguish Western worldviews and achievements from those of non-Western cultures, it may impede their ability to accept diversity with open minds and diminish their capacity to respond to change with imagination and resilience.

The Pillar of a Globalized General Education Curriculum: World Civilizations

Instructors' classroom experiences together with the results of studies such as Barrows (1981) confirm the necessity of taking a global approach to cultural literacy. The call to expand our students' visions of the world is being heard, and concerned educators in the nation's community colleges are responding. One of the most exciting developments is that more community colleges (and universities) are offering freshman- and sophomore-level world civilizations courses. In many instances, these courses have replaced the traditional Western civilization courses and are being used to meet college general education requirements.

One of the guiding principles of the world civilizations course is the belief that exposure of students to the contributions that various civilizations in the history of our planet have made to the global bank of human culture will significantly diminish ethnocentric attitudes. The course essentially seeks to introduce students to different ways of thinking about the world and presents Western civilization as one among many civilizations. One of the conspicuous benefits of a world civilizations course is that it provides students with valuable insights into the needs that culturally bind human beings together and the creativity, richness, and diversity of the human condition. The knowledge and understanding gained from studying the worldviews and life-styles of others, in addition to one's own, enrich students and better prepare them to rationally and conscientiously deal with the many challenges of living (and succeeding) in a global civilization. It might be said that the NEH recommendation could accomplish the same ends, but there is an important difference. Most colleges and universities offer world civilizations as a two-semester (eight semester hours) or a three-term (twelve term hours) sequence. The NEH sequence of courses on civilizations is extended over a period of three years and requires eighteen semester hours (twenty-seven term hours) to complete! If taught with sufficient geographical and cultural balance, a world civilization program is an effective and efficient way to foster a global perspective, and it is certainly much more practical for the community college general education curriculum. Completion of a world civilizations program might also be propitious to students who wish to further their education at a four-year institution and specialize in the study of one particular cultural tradition (for example, Western, East Asian, or Islamic) because it equips them with the attitudes and skills needed to overcome the negative effects of cultural conditioning.

Implementation of a world civilizations program is not without challenges. Issues about textbooks and content usually stand as formidable obstacles to a successful program. Instructors often contend, for example, that teaching a world civilizations course is an unwarranted burden for them and their students because of the excessive amount of material to be covered in such a course. Others assert that world civilizations can be nothing more than a watered-down and useless history course not only because of time constraints but also because most faculty do not possess expertise in non-Western areas. What is reflected in some of these instructional concerns is the attachment that many faculty have to the traditional comprehensive chronological approach to teaching history. That approach emphasizes "building block" content and assumes that there is a set body of information that every student should know (which may explain our fascination with lists, also). In a Western civilization course, for example, instructors systematically lay down the necessary Greco-Roman foundation and then proceed step by step, period by period, to build a kind of intellectual pyramid on which students can stand to view the world. This approach is futile for teaching world civilizations. One cannot expect to utilize the same methodology applied to teaching a Western or American civilization course for a world civilizations course. The instructional goals are different and their fulfillment necessitates a different methodology.

There are a number of workable models for teaching world civilizations employed in colleges and universities across the nation. One can be characterized as a diffusionist model. William H. McNeill, a nationally renowned historian from the University of Chicago, describes this approach in the preface of his book *A History of the Human Community*: "World history can and should be written to show how in succeeding ages different human groups achieved unusual creativity, and then impelled or compelled those around them (and, in time, across long distances) to alter their accustomed style of life to take account of the new things that had come to their attention by what anthropologists call 'cultural diffusion' from the center of creativity" (1990, p. xv).

The organizing idea of this model is simple. The primary focus of a world civilizations course in which this approach is used is on only those civilizations in world history that served as centers of extraordinary cultural creativity. At the same time, it draws students' attention to some of the ways in which surrounding peoples adopted, adapted, or rejected the values, beliefs, artistic styles, political innovations, technology, and so on associated with those centers. The diffusionist model can be effective in increasing the students' awareness of the interrelatedness of world civilizations through history. It is also especially convenient for colleges that have just made the curriculum transition from Western civilization to world civilizations because the emphasis is on patterns of relationships and not on an enormous amount of factual information characteristic of more historical approaches. Instructors need not be specialists in, and intimately familiar with, the seemingly infinite variety of cultural traditions throughout history. Furthermore, the Western chronological framework, to which faculty are accustomed, can easily be retained.

The approach of teaching world civilizations thematically is also efficacious. As two faculty members in humanities at Lansing Community College who developed a thematic model have explained, "One obvious solution to the pitfalls associated with the comprehensive-chronological instruction of World Civilizations is to recast the purpose and nature of the course by allowing for more in-depth focus on and analysis of particular topics or themes. This will make the course more manageable for instructors and students alike" (Sjoquist and Steck, 1991, p. 9).

This approach allows faculty to be creative in choice of topics and selective with regard to course material. With the thematic model utilized by these two instructors, course content is organized around what anthropologists call "universals of culture" (that is, cultural needs shared by all people at all times). Each world civilizations course employs three unit themes: providing order and security, adjusting to and assimilating advances in science and technology, and searching for and expressing ultimate truths and meaning in human existence. These themes easily allow for the critical examination and comparison of cultural components such as worldviews, artistic and literary trends, scientific and technological achievements, and political and social organizations. The instructors choose representative civilizations from Europe, Africa, Asia, and the Americas and examine and compare, for example, the ways in which these civilizations have responded to the need for order and security. They argue that the main advantage of using cultural universals as themes is that "they are timeless and remain as relevant today as centuries ago and thus are meaningful to contemporary students who personally identify with them and the related responses of their predecessors. They illustrate the oneness of the human experience, the common struggle faced by all civilizations, and help students overcome ethnocentrism and misoneism" (Sjoquist and Steck, 1991, p. 11).

With this particular thematic model, history becomes less abstract and more significant. The students' realization that the differences and similarities perceived in the study of world civilizations are rooted in shared cultural needs helps them to see the essential oneness of humankind.

The above represent only two feasible models for teaching world civilizations at the community college level. There are variations of these models and, of course, other models that are altogether distinct. What is important to remember, however, is that the world civilizations course is desirable for a general education curriculum, it is teachable, and it has proved to be successful.

Additional Requisites for a Globalized General Education Curriculum

One of the cornerstones of the globalized general education curriculum is world geography. Proficiency in geography and map usage is certainly not an unjustified requisite given the goals of the globalized curriculum and the documented geographical and cartographical nescience of American students. It is a course that complements the world civilizations sequence since students need to know where world civilizations are and were located in the world and which natural conditions may have affected the development and character of a civilization's political, economic, or even religious institutions and systems. The diffusion of ideas and technology, for instance, becomes much more understandable when one considers the role of geography. Perhaps no course provides a better means of introducing students to the idea of the interrelatedness of peoples.

At least one of the required science courses in the general education curriculum should address topics such as the international dimensions of the uses and abuses of the earth's natural resources and transnational pollution. These kinds of topics are relevant and lend themselves to the teaching of a global perspective. Other science courses could also devote more time to identifying the contributions of non-European and non-U.S. citizens to the field of science. How many of the students whom we teach can name a Third World scientist?

The Third Wave civilization requires students to be mathematically literate, and there should be little debate about whether or not a basic mathematics course belongs in the core curriculum. It does and it can enhance the students' global perspective. Instructors might examine the historical development of Western mathematics, for example, and analyze its relationship to religion, philosophy, the arts, and other sciences. Few students know, for example, that the numeration system they routinely use has Hindu-Arabic origins. Most of them are unaware of the cultural role that mathematics has played in various civilizations past and present. Discussion of a topic such as why Europeans were late in adopting the concept of zero and using negative numbers compared to other civilizations (for example Indian, Islamic, and Mayan) can nourish the students' appreciation for non-Western accomplishments and the contributions made to our own civilization.

In addition to writing courses, a world civilizations sequence, basic science and mathematics courses with a global perspective, and world geography, the community college should also consider other subjects. These might include comparative government, world literature, world religions, and foreign languages.

In a sense, a general education curriculum ceases to be "general" if it is dominated by one or two fields of study or is culture-specific. The core curriculum should reflect a balance of cultural traditions and disciplines and should serve to develop the kinds of literacies (for example, mathematical, geographical, and world cultural) that enhance the quality of life for all of us.

References

Barrows, T. S. *College Students' Knowledge and Beliefs: A Survey of Global Understanding: The Final Report of the Global Understanding Project*. New Rochelle, N.Y.: Change Magazine Press, 1981.

Cheney, L. V. *50 Hours: A Core Curriculum for College Students*. Washington, D.C.: National Endowment for the Humanities, 1989. 116 pp. (ED 308 804)

El-Khawas, E. H., Carter, D. J., and Ottinger, C. A. *Community College Fact Book*. New York: American Council on Education/Macmillan, 1988.

Hirsch, E. D., Jr. *Cultural Literacy: What Every American Needs to Know*. New York: Vintage Books, 1988.

McNeill, W. H. *A History of the Human Community*. Englewood Cliffs, N.J.: Prentice Hall, 1990.

Sjoquist, D. P., and Steck, D. E. *World Civilizations: A Thematic Approach*. East Lansing, Mich.: Third Wave, 1991.

Toffler, A. *Future Shock*. New York: Random House, 1970.

DOUGLAS P. SJOQUIST is associate professor of humanities and world civilizations studies at Lansing Community College, Lansing, Michigan.

The history, goals, and values of general and developmental education point to a common purpose. The two are so closely related, in fact, that both stand to benefit from a renewed and expanded cooperation.

General and Developmental Education: Finding Common Ground

Thomas L. Franke

Generic rationales for general education usually focus on the need for students to communicate effectively, think critically and solve problems, develop behavioral skills associated with educated persons, and cultivate the traits of responsible and involved citizenship, including familiarity with key elements of history and culture. Students do not, after all, major in general education. Even at the community college, where a liberal arts major does not necessarily identify a distinct specialty discipline, it is understood that the general education experience is preparatory to the major to be pursued after transfer. The participation of occupational students in general education coursework follows in part from the same rationale, except that the occupational specialty courses of the associate degree replace the major courses of the baccalaureate degree.

Definitions and Antecedents

Developmental education, according to the American Association of Community and Junior Colleges (1987, p. 1), has a similar focus on preparatory skills: "The term developmental education is used in postsecondary education to describe the programs that teach academically underprepared students the skills they need to be more successful learners. The term includes, but is not limited to, remedial courses."

Early developmental education efforts seem to have stressed the same basic skills—English (writing), reading, and mathematics—as similar programs do today. For example, Maxwell (1979, p. 8) notes that in the 1860s "Iowa State College required that entering freshmen be fourteen years old and able to read, write and do arithmetic." Nineteenth-century college entrance tests provided the impetus both for preparatory courses and for one of today's staple components of the general education program: freshman composition. When, for the 1873–1874 school year, Harvard announced that "each candidate will be required to write a short English composition, correct in spelling, punctuation, grammar, and expression" (Applebee, 1974, p. 30), it defined a focus for preparatory composition courses that is still familiar today. That year, "Harvard first offered freshman English at the request of faculty members who were dissatisfied with students' preparation in formal writing" (Maxwell, 1979, p. 8).

Another common general education component, the study of literature in English, entered the curriculum in part under the aegis of concern over students' writing skills. Novels and plays were considered by some nineteenth-century educators to be corrupting influences on young minds, and Oberlin College, for example, "refused to allow Shakespeare to be taught in mixed classes until the 1860s" (Applebee, 1974, p. 22). The influence of college entrance tests and freshman composition courses, however, prevailed, and "literature gained its foothold in the requirements through the nonliterary uses to which readings could be put" (Applebee, 1974, p. 30). Eventually, literature would be valued in its own right as a general education subject that cultivates cultural understanding, critical thinking, and aesthetic appreciation.

If the reading of English and American literature had its start in American education as a kind of hybrid of developmental and general education, it may be that a similar process is currently under way in the area of mathematics education. There is an increasing awareness of the need for mathematics competence, partly as a result of widespread use of new technologies and their associated methods in a variety of careers. A national survey revealed that 26 percent of freshmen at two-year colleges enroll in remedial mathematics courses, a higher percentage than in either reading or writing (Mansfield, Farris, and Black, 1991). Furthermore, enrollments do not adequately convey the magnitude of the mathematical skills crisis among today's students. The New Jersey Basic Skills Council (1989, p. 30) found that only 17 percent of the state's entering community college students were proficient in computation, and that a meager 4 percent were proficient in elementary algebra. Although it is possible to define the needs of 80 to 90 percent of entering students as remedial, there comes a point at which the definition must confront the reality of its users. As colleges raise their expectations and institute general education requirements for students in mathematics, we may see course content once considered "precollege" level for majors becoming credit-bearing general education work for the broader population.

Current Applications Combining General and Developmental Education

While general education has discovered skills, developmental education has discovered content. Issues related to content in developmental and general education are complex, but by viewing learning as a complex interaction of the learner and the environment, that is, by adopting a cognitive perspective, developmentalists are encouraged to incorporate content that taps the whole learner. The same influence seems to have led general education to elevate the thought processes (that is, skills) involved in the learning of content. Thus, as developmental education moves from a skills base and general education moves from a content base, the two approach one another toward the center of the skills-content continuum.

An example of the new trend in developmental education is Project Bridge at Laney College in Oakland, California. "Project Bridge is a community college program for remedial students who are so unprepared for academic work that they are often considered beyond hope educationally" (Griffith, Jacobs, Wilson, and Dashiell, 1988, p. 288). Suggestive of the earlier preparatory school concept, Project Bridge "creates a school within a school" (p. 288). However, the academic content of Project Bridge is far removed from the isolated skills approach, which Griffith, Jacobs, Wilson, and Dashiell say creates "a vicious cycle of non-achievement: year after year, basic skills students are kept away from ideas until they become 'more skilled.' But they do not become more skilled because they are kept from ideas" (p. 289).

Griffith, Jacobs, Wilson, and Dashiell (1988) do not accept the premise that the developmental student is merely "skill deficient." Instead, they posit that "there are various stages of studenthood . . . of readiness to function in academic settings" (p. 291). This holistic view of students incorporates a wide range of social and cultural characteristics into the teaching and learning process. The approach in Project Bridge includes four strategies: student-centered classrooms, emphasis on spoken language, inclusion of minority group cultures, and attention to information about the world. These strategies recognize that developmental students are often not familiar with the culture of higher education learning communities and must be introduced to it systematically, starting from the students' own backgrounds and abilities. By building on the strengths of the students' cultural backgrounds—for example, in spoken language performance, even when such language performance may not initially fit traditional academic patterns— Project Bridge meets students at their own points of entrance to higher education and builds skills within the context of a larger and more complex cultural process of attaining "studenthood." This process is similar to that implicit in traditional general education programs, except that the starting point is different.

Although Project Bridge recognizes the importance of skills development and includes courses in reading, writing, and mathematics, it coordinates skill building with content courses. Bridge content courses have been developed "in biology, chemistry, sociology, humanities, ethnic studies, and computer science" (Griffith, Jacobs, Wilson, and Dashiell, 1988, p. 295). Aside from the students in them, how do these courses differ from standard general education courses in the same subjects? First, reading, writing, and computing skills appropriate to the students' entry levels are systematically woven into the courses. In addition, the courses "make . . . ideas accessible to students who read poorly" (p. 295). Further, the bridge content courses "base the acquisition of knowledge on the students' non-academic experience . . . [and] result in a student product" (p. 295). These products are often collaborative in nature, class projects rather than individual projects produced by students in isolation. In other regards, the bridge course goals parallel those of general education courses. For example, they "present significant ideas in the respective discipline . . . [and] encourage the student to think analytically" (p. 295).

Although not yet a widespread phenomenon, the creation of developmental content courses is occurring at other community colleges. Schoolcraft College (1989), for example, offers developmental courses in biology, chemistry, drafting, and physics. In an approach that places less emphasis on the acquisition of specific bodies of information, Lansing Community College offers "Natural Science 100, which incorporates material appropriate for the underprepared and science-anxious student" (Brown and Cranson, 1989, p. 32). It is noteworthy that proposed revisions to the general education science courses at Lansing would shift emphasis from content acquisition to process skills. Thus, Lansing's Science Department reflects the converging trends of developmental and general education toward a common ground, as described earlier.

At Lansing Community College, a mixture of decentralized (departmental) and centralized approaches exists. Although developmental mathematics and science courses are offered by their discipline-based departments, several years ago the Department of Academic Enrichment Services was created to assume responsibility for developmental instruction in reading, writing, and English as a second language.

Recognizing that the existing array of courses based on specific skills did not address the broad academic needs of students, Steven Hopkins (1988) developed an integrated core developmental language skills curriculum. Hopkins's design calls for an academic preparation sequence, a series of three courses that introduces students to the experience of working in a learning community while developing reading, writing, speaking, and listening skills. As in Project Bridge, students start with exploration of their own experiences but begin to relate personal and family experiences to a wider knowledge gleaned from fellow students as well as from sources external to the college. In the second course, students focus on the language of college assignments in a wide variety of disciplines, and, in the third course, critical thinking is introduced on the assumption that such thinking is a prerequisite to college-level general education courses. In developing the courses of the academic preparation sequence, faculty went to each of the departments offering general education courses and asked them to help identify the abilities that students should bring with them to their general education work. The goal of this ongoing collaboration is to arrive at a consensus definition of the dividing line between developmental and general education and to design a smooth transition for students from one level to the other.

At this point, faculty involved in the academic preparation sequence expect to retain individual courses in reading and writing on the assumption that some students will not require the complete integrated package. However, even in these stand-alone courses, the movement away from isolated skills is apparent. A course in which grammar and mechanics were formerly taught as isolated skills has become a composition course with reading included. The reading clinic, which serves students reading below the seventh-grade level, still provides assistance with specific skills, but it also incorporates National Issues Forums in which students discuss and debate content that is of both personal and public concern. Reading clinic students use books "written at the 4.5–6.5 reading level. . . . [But] all the basic arguments of the original NIF [National Issues Forums] text are included" (National Issues Forums, 1990, p. 8).

As these examples indicate, developmental education is moving away from the simplistic basic skills hierarchy in which mechanical skills precede content. As general education increases its emphasis on enhancing thinking skills rather than defining specific information to be learned, the distinctions between developmental and general education fade. In the best realization of these trends, there will not be two programs at all but instead a single learning sequence with a somewhat arbitrarily set line between pre-college- and college-level work. On one side of the line will be developmental education, on the other general education, but students should feel no shock upon crossing that line.

Steps to Create Common Ground

The current relationship between developmental and general education should be close and mutually supportive. Both areas are in some respects "service" areas to the rest of higher education. Developmental educators can bring general educators a familiarity with cross-curriculum approaches based on reading in the content areas, writing across the curriculum, or mathematics for technical applications. By contrast, Campbell and Wood (1987, p. 69) note that "most general education efforts are strongly departmentalized, with little training of faculty in the development of interdisciplinary courses." This departmentalization and tradition of discipline-based approaches often subvert change in general education and prevent it from establishing a productive dialogue with the occupational programs in community colleges. The importance and value of such dialogue is well illustrated by the findings of the Shared Vision Task Force (1991), which focused on the humanities in occupational education and recommended that "colleges work to create an understanding and appreciation of the mutually supportive aims of humanities and occupational education among the faculty and the professional staff" (p. 22). Because developmental educators routinely work with both liberal arts and occupational faculty and students, they are in a good position to facilitate this essential dialogue.

As developmental education is freed from a narrow skills focus, general education faculty can provide important insights into the higher-order thinking processes that must be initiated even in the early phases of the developmental sequence. General education faculty can share teaching techniques that tap higher-order processes and can help developmental educators identify and fill the gap that often exists between the developmental sequence and the introductory general education courses. This gap, one of the most dangerous faced by many students, must be filled if the developmental program is to have maximum impact on student success and retention. At the same time, developmental educators have devised a variety of student-centered teaching strategies that could be used to energize general education courses.

Ideally, all or most of the developmental and the general educators would work occasionally in each other's domain. Developmental educators who never teach general education courses can easily lose sight of their students' future needs. General education faculty who never teach developmental courses may never appreciate the alternative learning styles of developmental students and of the effective techniques that have been devised for work with them.

Crossover teaching between the two domains may be most easily accomplished by teachers in disciplines such as English and mathematics. Should sociologists, philosophers, and computer scientists teach developmental courses as well? Where developmental content courses are involved, they should, although care must be taken to select content specialists who respect underprepared students and are willing to adopt new teaching techniques. Most promising are approaches in which developmental and general education faculty work together. Pairing of courses, for example, encourages teamwork and learning while respecting individual expertise. In this model, the same students simultaneously enroll in specific developmental and general education courses. The work of the developmental English class may be the paper assigned by the history professor. The English professor focuses on the reading and writing strategies needed for success in the history course, while the history professor focuses on the history content per se. Inevitably, however, this division is not absolute. As the two faculty members work together, each learns about the other's concerns and, most important, about the needs of the students in the paired courses. This same approach could be used to link developmental, general, and occupational courses.

While course pairing is a worthwhile strategy, it does not address a larger issue: the establishment of a college culture. Gaff (1989) calls for a second wave of general education reform, the key to which, he argues, is the establishment of "a college culture marked by a coherent set of values" (p. 14). Citing the example of major corporations, he declares that "the essential first step for a college, like a corporation, is to decide what it stands for by way of undergraduate education" (p. 14). Both general and developmental education have essential roles in creating and implementing such an institutional commitment. It would be unfortunate indeed if developmental and general educators chose anything other than a close and supportive relationship. In fact, if we allow ourselves to think of general education beyond the boundaries of academic disciplines, we inescapably come to realize that developmental and general education combine to form a whole that is more valuable and desirable than its separate parts.

References

American Association of Community and Junior Colleges. *Policy Statement: Developmental Education Programs.* Washington, D.C.: American Association of Community and Junior Colleges, 1987.

Applebee, A. N. *Tradition and Reform in the Teaching of English: A History.* Urbana, Ill.: National Council of Teachers of English, 1974.

Brown, M. H., and Cranson, K. R. "Science Anxiety and the Community College Student." *Journal of College Science Teaching,* 1989, *19* (1), 30–33.

Campbell, D. F., and Wood, M. T. "General Education in the Occupational Curriculum: Why? To What Extent? With What Results?" In C. R. Doty (ed.), *Developing Occupational Programs.* New Directions for Community Colleges, no. 58. San Francisco: Jossey-Bass, 1987.

Gaff, J. G. "General Education at Decade's End: The Need for a Second Wave of Reform." *Change,* 1989, *21* (4), 10–19.

Griffith, M., Jacobs, B., Wilson, S., and Dashiell, M. "Changing the Model: Working with Underprepared Students." *Community/Junior College Quarterly of Research and Practice,* 1988, *12* (4), 287–303.

Hopkins, S. *Proposal for the Department of Academic Enrichment Services.* Lansing, Mich.: Lansing Community College, 1988.

Mansfield, W., Farris, E., and Black, M. *College-Level Remedial Education in the Fall of 1989: Survey Report.* Washington, D.C.: National Center for Education Statistics, 1991. 65 pp. (ED 323 630)

Maxwell, M. *Improving Student Learning Skills: A Comprehensive Guide to Successful Practices and Programs for Increasing the Performance of Underprepared Students.* San Francisco: Jossey-Bass, 1979.

National Issues Forums. *Leadership Handbook, 1990–91.* Dayton, Ohio: National Issues Forums, 1990.

New Jersey Basic Skills Council. *Report to the New Jersey Board of Higher Education on the Results of the New Jersey College Basic Skills Placement Testing.* Trenton: New Jersey State Department of Higher Education, 1989. 102 pp. (ED 305 867)

Schoolcraft College. *General Education Goals.* Livonia, Mich.: Schoolcraft College, 1989.

Shared Vision Task Force. *Successfully Integrating the Humanities into Associate Degree Occupational Programs: An Implementation Manual.* Wausau, Wisc.: Community College Humanities Association and the National Council for Occupational Education, 1991. 101 pp. (ED 330 405)

THOMAS L. FRANKE *is chair of the Department of Academic Enrichment Services and acting vice president for academic and student affairs at Lansing Community College, Lansing, Michigan.*

Although community colleges have become the major point of entry into higher education for America's minorities, there are serious questions concerning their effectiveness as a base for the transfer and career paths of these students. What changes need to be made in general education to ensure greater success for minorities?

General Education for At-Risk Students

Laura I. Rendón, Janyth Fredrickson

In this decade, perhaps higher education's greatest challenge is to determine how to educate a new generation of students, the most diverse ever, in order to help them find a common ground with each other and become leaders who will bring us closer together in spite of our differences. The general education task gives rise to challenging issues. How should community colleges deal with the dynamic growth of people of color, who once occupied only peripheral roles in our society? How do we come to terms with and integrate new languages, cultures, and customs that we barely understand without sacrificing the rich, individual nuances of diverse cultures? How can community colleges help these new groups of students achieve their educational and social goals?

A Proposal to Guide General Education

Boyer and Levine (1981) present a useful perspective that community colleges may adopt to develop a general education program. Avoiding the mere listing of courses to prescribe the general education curriculum, Boyer and Levine propose six broad categories of study that flow across the curriculum. They are (1) our use of symbols for communication, (2) shared membership in groups and institutions, (3) interdependence of production and consumption, (4) our relationship with nature, (5) our use of time, and (6) our shared beliefs and values. By embracing these six categories, a community college may emerge with a solid conceptual foundation on which to build a general education program. According to Boyer and Levine, general education should give attention to shared experiences, focus on areas of interdependence, and concentrate on the collection of activities that knit isolated individuals into a community.

NEW DIRECTIONS FOR COMMUNITY COLLEGES, no. 81, Spring 1993   © Jossey-Bass Publishers

The important thing to remember is that these six categories are essential to what constitutes an educated person. Whether they are incorporated into a list of courses within a major, incorporated into an experimental general education college within a community college, or brought together in other creative configurations is left to individual colleges to decide. Boyer and Levine's model is used here to provide a perspective, a guide that community colleges may use to develop a general education program for at-risk students while also preparing minority and majority students to function in a world that is increasingly interdependent as well as in an American society that is becoming increasingly multicultural.

Shared Use of Symbols for Communication

Boyer and Levine's first category involves reading with understanding, writing with clarity, and listening and speaking effectively. It also involves developing proficiency in the use of numbers as an essential and universally accepted symbol system. In addition to these most basic skills, the category is expanded to include cultural, technical, and artistic communication. Without this broad foundation in receiving, processing, and sending meaningful communication in a variety of media, students are educationally crippled with respect to participation in further study. Without cultural training, they cannot participate fully in our pluralistic society. While these diverse topics are frequently taught in isolated courses, the most effective approaches integrate targeted skills in every class.

The use of writing across the curriculum, for example, provides for the wide application of communications skills. At Durham Technical Community College in North Carolina, students in mathematics classes respond subjectively to classwork through daily writings. Although writing was once eschewed as irrelevant, students now agree that it helps them clarify abstract concepts and pinpoint problem areas. In Arizona, the Maricopa Writing Project draws together faculty from diverse disciplines each summer to share ideas about writing across the curriculum (Roueche and Roueche, 1989).

Critical thinking, synthesis, and analysis are other basic skills that at-risk students must learn well to succeed in higher education. Often, the material is found in advanced reading courses for developmental studies, but it can also be presented in a series of skills workshops or freshmen seminars. Once learned, basic approaches to processing information transcend a single subject and stretch across the curriculum from laboratory sciences to literature. An understanding of and sensitivity to other cultures also needs to spill across the curriculum. In essence, the study of a second culture and language serves as a two-way mirror: Students are able to look through the glass at another perspective as well as see the reflection of their own from a different angle. The European-centered, Great Books approach to general education ignores the significant contributions of minority scholars in history, science, and literature. Study must reflect the extraordinary pluralism of our culture. The National Technical Institute for the Deaf has an elective cluster on "heritage" that is team-taught by culturally knowledgeable instructors from different disciplines (Gaff, 1981).

Finally, all students must be prepared for the age of technology. Hands-on use of a computer and a broad understanding of its capability should be incorporated into the overlapping curriculum. Cuyahoga Community College's Metropolitan Campus in Ohio loans laptop computers to its students and has discovered that writing skills have improved as a result (Shaw, 1989). Students at Johnson County Community College in Kansas learn how to write as they learn word processing (Anandam, 1989).

Shared Membership in Groups and Institutions

With their second category, Boyer and Levine (1981, p. 33) emphasize that "general education . . . would look at the origin of institutions; how they evolve, grow strong, become oppressive or weak, and sometimes die. It would examine . . . how institutions work, explore the interaction between institutions and individuals, and show how such interaction both facilitates and complicates our existence." Numerous methodologies may be employed to focus on this category in different disciplines. LaGuardia Community College in New York developed a cluster of disciplines around the theme of work in society and its impact on the individual (Matthews, 1986), and other possibilities abound. With initial guidance, student groups can design simple research projects to conduct outside the classroom with other students and members of the community. Discussions focusing on commonalities as well as conflicts can help students examine their own group affiliations as they begin to see shared needs.

Students can target a single group for close examination. The group can be a community-based organization such as the League of United Latin American Citizens, Bureau of Indian Affairs, or a black church. Students can also examine the culture of the barrio, ghetto, or reservation. A likely outcome of this type of project is the integration of information and skills and a greater understanding of how new social structures shape lives, set policy, restrict choices, and provide services to people on the margins of society.

Shared Production and Consumption

The third category explores the significance of work, a form of both consumption and production, as well as how work patterns reflect the values and shape the social climate of a culture. Cedar Valley College in Texas has identified an almost identical theme in its skills-for-living approach to general education. One of the themes explored concerns the roles and functions of the worker, the consumer, and the citizen (Clowes, Lukenbill, and Shaw, 1979). This theme easily lends itself to minority and majority perspectives.

Fieldwork can also help bring this far-ranging theme from an abstract to a personal level. Students can develop the framework to examine their families' roles in producing and consuming. And because so many of community college students work themselves, their own involvement should be considered. This category, too, can help students realistically assess their own situations. How do their career goals compare to the reality of the moment? Are the goals realistically attainable—and desirable? And what are the steps to reach them? Interviews with working professionals could focus on revealing differences between blue- and white-collar jobs, fields in which minorities are, respectively, the most and least represented, as well as on the barriers experienced by minorities attempting to climb social and career ladders and strategies to overcome these barriers.

Global questions should address effects of consumption and production on our planet. National boundaries will begin to fade as students explore the use and misuse of resources on a global scale. In so doing, students should begin to realize that we are all members of a single interconnected group.

Shared Relationship with Nature

Boyer and Levine's fourth category suggests a general education that introduces students to the application of scientific methodologies and facts and how these relate to citizenship. To set a foundation for this framework of study, an awareness of the scientific method of inquiry is essential. In laboratory science classes, experimentation is essential, and students should be required to create their own experiments, regardless of outcomes, to understand the process of discovery. Classroom assignments can include writing to trace the consequences of trial and error over a period of time. In nonscience majors, students can focus on our shared relationship with nature by writing papers on contemporary topics such as the effects of prescribed drugs and illegal drugs, disease and aging, and AIDS on our entire society and the impact of the Exxon Valdez oil spill on the Alaska ecological system. These broad topics can also be examined through group assignments, research papers, or interaction with practicing scientists.

The result of this approach will be students who are better aware of the power of science and of society's potential to use knowledge for great good or great harm. Two examples show the many possibilities for integrating science with other disciplines for a general education curriculum. Jackson State University in Mississippi has created the two-semester course Literature of Science, taught by an English instructor, which draws students from across the curriculum, including those in the fine arts. Reading takes the spotlight in this sequential course, which stretches from the beginnings of science to

Einstein and ecology. Tuskegee Institute in Alabama created three science courses for nonmajors that focus on human biology and the interrelationships of physical sciences (Parler, 1982).

Shared Use of Time

The fifth category advances an awareness of the confluences of events that have shaped our past, our present, and our options for the future. This is our "history" in the broadest sense, an intricate weaving of many threads, both mighty and mundane, with the pattern only partially finished.

In approaching this theme, the content of history must be reconceptualized. Too often, history symbolizes an endless list of definitions and dates that seem irrelevant to students' lives and is peopled only by Anglo-European political figures and warriors. The challenge, then, is to make history matter, to help students understand its relevance to all students, minority and majority, male and female. An important step is to carefully choose learning themes in which minorities and women have played a central role, such as the Vietnam War, the civil rights movement, the struggle for women's liberation, and farm workers' strikes.

As in the other categories of Boyer and Levine's (1981) model, one of the best ways to instill appreciation of history is to let students discover it themselves in a hands-on manner, and a good place to start is at home. One assignment can involve recording of the oral histories of elderly family members. Another approach is to ask students to research the migration of their ancestors and the life-styles of the first generation in the United States. This will help students realize that we share an immigrant heritage.

Other countries' cultural patterns and differences should also be studied. Queens College of the City University of New York offers a strong foundation in Western culture and then study of the cultures of other continents (Cheney, 1989). Our Latin neighbors to the south deserve a closer look through a two-way mirror. Practically every community has recent immigrants from Central America or Mexico. Students should share their living histories to supplement the text. The result will be a better appreciation of our shared humanity as well as students' closer appreciation of their own origins.

Shared Beliefs and Values

The last category concerns the examination of distinctions between beliefs and facts and of how values are formed, transmitted, and revised. As the culmination of their general education, at-risk students should emerge with a growing sense of their personal identities and values as well as an understanding of the ethical principles of our society. The traditional disciplines that these topics broach include philosophy and ethics, religion, and anthropology, but practically every field has room to incorporate the formulation of values, decisions, and ethical and moral choices. Faculty will have to exercise care so that their courses allow students to articulate, clarify, and defend the premises of their belief systems. For example, in a sociology course, time should be allowed for students to discuss the meaning of diversity and whether our society really celebrates or disdains it. In a history course, students should define words such as democracy, equality, capitalism, and freedom. As a society, do our actions match our words? Individual considerations should also be discussed. What values guide how diverse groups live their lives? What values are held in common by fellow students regardless of ethnic background and socioeconomic level? And what are the implications for society of values that are not shared? North Seattle Community College has created an interdisciplinary program called American Values to examine similar topics (Shaw, 1989).

Conclusion

Perhaps the most significant social force shaping our nation is the dynamic growth of people of color. New people bring fresh challenges and fertile opportunities. The general education program represents a vehicle for focusing on the creation of fully educated persons. At-risk students should not be held to minimal expectations. They must be afforded the opportunity to fully develop all of their capacities—to communicate clearly, to think logically and critically, to get along with different types of people, and to work independently and as team members.

References

Anandam, K. "Expanding Horizons for Learning and Technology." In T. O'Banion (ed.), *Innovation in the Community College.* New York: American Council on Education/Macmillan, 1989.

Boyer, E. L., and Levine, A. "A Quest for Common Learning." *Change,* 1981, *13* (3), 28–35.

Cheney, L. V. *50 Hours: A Core Curriculum for College Students.* Washington, D.C.: National Endowment for the Humanities, 1989. 116 pp. (ED 308 804)

Clowes, D. A., Lukenbill, J. D., and Shaw, R. G. "General Education in the Community College: A Search for Purpose." Paper presented at the annual meeting of the American Association of Community and Junior Colleges, Chicago, April 29–May 2, 1979. 25 pp. (ED 192 832)

Gaff, J. "Reconstructing General Education: Lessons from Project GEM." *Change,* 1981, *13* (6), 52–56.

Matthews, R. "Learning Communities in the Community College: How to Improve Student Involvement and Raise Faculty Morale." *Community, Junior, and Technical College Journal,* 1986, *57* (2), 44–47.

Parler, N. P. *Improving Minority Students' Competencies: Strategies in Selected Colleges.* Atlanta, Ga.: Southern Regional Education Board, 1982. 88 pp. (ED 221 145)

Roueche, S. D., and Roueche, J. E. "Innovations in Teaching: The Past as Prologue." In T.

O'Banion (ed.), *Innovation in the Community College*. New York: American Council on Education/Macmillan, 1989.

Shaw, R. G. "Change in the Community College: Pendulum Swing or Spiral Soar?" In T. O'Banion (ed.), *Innovation in the Community College*. New York: American Council on Education/Macmillan, 1989.

LAURA I. RENDÓN *is associate professor in the Division of Educational Leadership and Policy Studies at Arizona State University, Tempe.*

JANYTH FREDRICKSON *is associate dean and department head of college transfer at Durham Technical College, Durham, North Carolina.*

Changes in the workplace are occurring at a pace that will force vocational education and general education to create new approaches and a new integration of efforts where enmity had previously existed. If this integration is to be successful, six specific general education demands must be met.

Vocational Education and General Education: New Relationship or Shotgun Marriage?

James Jacobs

It is now conventional wisdom at gatherings of vocational educators to call for more linkage between vocational and academic education. In addition, the Carl D. Perkins Vocational and Applied Technology Act of 1990, which is the major federal legislation that defines and organizes vocational education, mandates that all state plans for vocational education must measure "student progress in the achievement of basic and more advanced academic skills" (part B, section 115). The establishment of a dialogue between vocational education and general education is a welcome development in postsecondary education. However, what is most important to understand is that this new interaction has been prompted by an *external* force: the changing skill needs of American business.

Business Skill Needs in the New Era

In the past decade, American higher education has been increasingly forced to define a new role in its relationship to the private sector. Once again, there has been a call for American higher education to serve the interests of U.S. businesses. This is not a new development. Since the late nineteenth century, there have been a number of movements that have called for greater ties between business and education (Kazis, 1988). This time the major thrust has been for American colleges and universities to aid in the training and education needs of American corporations. This has made it necessary for education staff to discuss the intermeshing of business skill needs and the education delivery system. What is missing from many of these discussions is the realization that not only has the absolute *magnitude* of skill deficits and corresponding needs for education and training increased but so too has the *qualitative nature* of those needed skills and instructional services.

Perhaps the major factor contributing to changes in the qualitative nature of skill and training needs has been the rapidly accelerating pace of technological change, particularly in durable goods manufacturing. Changes in manufacturing processes and systems tend to have wide and pervasive implications for skill needs in the work force. Over the past ten to fifteen years, industries have dramatically changed their capital stock as well as the level of technology embedded in their products, leading to a transformation on the shop floor. Most of these changes have involved the computerization of specific machines and functions, as well as the linking together of computer-controlled devices into increasingly complex computer-integrated manufacturing systems.

These dramatic changes in the technological landscape of manufacturing are producing corresponding changes in the skills needed in workers. Moreover, these skill changes and the new manufacturing technologies have a social-technical impact. In order to realize the productivity-enhancing potential of the new technologies, companies have had to adapt them to their organizational settings. This has often involved extensive changes in job descriptions and guidelines. Moreover, there have been fairly dramatic changes in the structures and processes of the manufacturing organization, which have increased the need for individuals who can initiate actions and respond creatively to situations, not simply follow orders. The new technologies demand more of the same basic skills that were used in the old jobs, with the old technology. For example, Jacobs and McAlinden (1991), studying the skill shifts associated with programmable machining and assembly technologies in manufacturing, found changes in needed verbal and mathematics skills that were both technology-specific as well as technology-generic. Nonetheless, the more challenging shifts in skill needs have been associated with technology-induced alterations of jobs and organizations. For example, Majchrzak (1985) studied the implementation of several computer-based technologies in manufacturing settings. She found that each technology tended to have its own signature of associated shifts in cognitive skills, job definitions, and organizational changes; all areas addressed form a general education base.

Skills and the Workplace

More to the concern of community college educators, the dimension of skill has been extended beyond the issue of technical skills. Many policymakers within job training programs, as well as researchers who survey employers, believe that "employability" skills are growing in significance, along with the need for critical basic skills in mathematics, reading, and writing (Carnevale and Gainer, 1989). A major survey of twenty-seven hundred Michigan employers who were asked to rank in significance eighty-six separate skills (divided into academic, personal management, and teamwork categories) found that five of the seven skills rated the highest were in the area of personal management such as "be free from substance abuse, demonstrate honesty and integrity, show respect for others" (Mehrens, 1989, p. 17).

The new manufacturing technologies present challenges to community college vocational education in a number of ways. First, the main thrust of industry has been to retrain the present work force. One major response of community colleges has been the development of customized or contracted training. These are classes taught by institutions for business clients that may incorporate some of the material of traditional classes but are expressly designed to serve the needs of the businesses involved. Often they are taught without any college credit given. Many times these courses are offered on the site of the employer.

There has been an unprecedented growth in the demands for customized training courses. For example, in the state of Illinois, employee training conducted by community colleges affected twenty-two thousand individuals from 900 companies in 1985. Two years later, the same schools served over thirty-seven thousand students and 1,395 companies (Illinois Community College Board, 1987). In Michigan, while the number of students in traditional vocational education courses declined by 8 percent in the period 1984–1987, a survey of customized training units indicated a 56 percent increase in the period 1981–1988 (Jacobs, 1989).

The growth of customized training appears to contradict the conventional definition of vocational education, that is, to give students skills for entry-level work. Students in customized training classes already possess jobs. They want to be trained either in new skills to maintain their present jobs or in skills that lead to job advancement. Indeed, the distinction between training and education is blurring as firms and workers demand skill-specific training and general knowledge of technical areas. Moreover, since most of these workers have been out of school for many years, they are often in need of traditional courses in communication and mathematical skills before they are able to undertake technical training. Thus, there is a demand for general education within the general process of customized technical training.

The mixture between general education and vocational courses has become further intertwined by the development of jointly funded union-management training programs. Typically, these are programs that provide funds for unionized workers to take courses—often on-site—that encompass both technical training and job enrichment. In many cases, the rank-and-file select courses in general education subjects, such as English or a social science, before selecting the technical training. In addition, some colleges have begun to offer credit for general education courses that are "industrially specific," that is, they are taught using subject matter that is related to an industry (Phelps, Brandenburg, and Jacobs, 1990).

Six New General Education Demands for Vocational Education

Successful integration of vocational and general education depends on the satisfaction of six key demands. First, the critical thinking skills that come from the general education curriculum are central to the successful implementation of technologies such as computer-automated design (CAD). If the main demand for vocational education now comes from the workplace, then some course components need to deal with problems of implementing a technology, as well as with the skills associated with its operation. The conventional course of study in vocational education tends to teach skills that permit an individual to operate a piece of equipment or set of interrelated equipment. One can learn to be a CAD operator at most community colleges and develop sufficient skills to perform most two-dimensional drawings. However, if a firm is to realize significant productivity gains from CAD, it requires an understanding of how the process can be applied to making libraries of parts, to storing and manipulating CAD-generated information, and to passing those data to other machines, such as cutting tools. These needs make it incumbent that the CAD operator understand how the technology fits within the production strategy of the firm, a topic that too few CAD courses cover (Arnsdorf and Jacobs, 1990).

Second, basic skills need to be part of the vocational education program. New manufacturing technologies call for more attention to the use of basic skills to compute, deduce, and communicate answers to problems. The concern for basic skills at the workplace has already been amply demonstrated by both industrial and government sources (Chisman, 1989). What is less well understood is how these skills can be integrated within the present technical training performed in vocational education courses. Teaching in most vocational education classes is based on repetition and observation of others; this is a useful approach, but it needs to be coupled with basic skills concepts. It is disturbing that such subjects as mathematics are segregated from vocational education programs and are taught only by general education faculty.

Third, the ability to grow and change is required in the workplace. Basic skills are especially important because the applications of new manufacturing technologies to particular problems are extremely diverse. There is not one way to implement computer numerical control. In some firms, the programming of the machine is undertaken by the engineering department, far removed from the shop floor. In other firms, program adjustments are made by the operator of the equipment. Which is the most advantageous method depends on the specific strategy of the firm. However, if firms are to realize greater flexibility than what computer-based technologies bring to the workplace, workers must possess broad general skills and the ability to learn and adjust skills at the workplace. Indeed, the Committee for Economic Development, a national association of business groups, has been critical of vocational education: "Business in general is not interested in narrow vocationalism. In many aspects, business believes that the schools in recent years have strayed too far in that direction. For most students, employers would prefer a curriculum that stresses literacy, mathematical skills, and problem-solving skills; one that emphasizes learning how to learn and adapting to change" (1985, p. 15).

Fourth, workers must be able to integrate basic skills with the shifts in workplace and market demands. New manufacturing technologies certainly decrease the amount of direct labor involved in manufacturing, but they raise the demand for associated work. The repair and maintenance function, for example, becomes increasingly critical (McAlinden, 1989). There are many tasks related to software development, positioning of machine vision systems, and quality control of operations. All of these tasks are performed by skilled workers, often those upgraded from production work. The challenge to vocational educators is to develop programs that train workers in the skills necessary to advance along what has been termed the "labor queue" (Piore and Sabel, 1984). Within this conception of career paths, the possession of basic learning skills is a key to successful movement within the firm. Thus, a combination of basic skills as well as knowledge of the internal labor market of firms are important for successful community college vocational programs.

Fifth, community college vocational educators need to relearn and update their own knowledge and skills. The new manufacturing technologies present a dual challenge to vocational education administrations in that they often require both new equipment and staff development. In most community colleges, the faculty in the vocational education area received their technical training in the premicrocomputer era, and unless adequate staff development plans have been in place, they have probably lagged behind the development of the technology. DePietro and others' (1989) study of exemplary vocational education programs found that many community colleges have purchased modern equipment, but few have undertaken the staff development necessary to teach advanced manufacturing technologies.

Community college educators do not understand the skills that current workers really need to work with the new technologies. But, equally significant, staff tend to approach technical training as one would teach skills to inexperienced youth. What might be appropriate for an eighteen-year-old just out of high school and looking for a trade is not suitable for students in their midthirties, most of whom already have jobs and attend class in the evenings. These learners each have a work history, family, and context around which good technical training must be built. In short, they need to be taught in a style that can draw out their own skills.

Sixth, workers need to expand their skills to include information gathering, analytical and critical thinking abilities, and decision making. The introduction of new technology is associated with the broader issue of organizational change within business in the United States. Corporations are moving away from an era of mass production to one of specialization and marketing (Piore and Sabel, 1984). Thus, the principal strength of a business organization is not the ability to realize economies of scale and produce cheaper goods than its competitors but rather skill in recognizing trends in the market and quickly responding with targeted products and services. For example, a successful automobile company does not design cars for the general American family but rather, based on marketing information, for different segments of that family, that is, professionals without children, retired couples, and so on. Products are fashioned to suit the needs and tastes of subunits and thus to sell in lower volumes, but in a rich diversity of models. From this perspective, the reason that the Japanese automobile makers have done so well in the United States is not because their costs are lower but because they have geared their production strategies to make quick product adjustments to meet changing consumer tastes.

This emphasis on flexibility and quick responses to the marketplace tends to alter the skills necessary for success. Information gathering, analytical and critical thinking skills, and decision making take on heightened importance, not only for the top management of the company but for all levels of the organization. Indeed, the successful firms build less hierarchical organizations and strive to bring decision making close to the production process. The skills that are necessary to provide leadership for the company are the same as those needed on the shop floor: flexibility, analytical thinking, and the ability to manipulate information. Not only do all of these imply higher levels of work skills, they also need to be learned in a different way from that in the past.

Crisis in Vocational Education

Because of these changes, traditional vocational education has experienced a profound crisis that calls for the attention of those in general education as well. While liberal arts instructors and administrators often seem under siege from the increasing vocationalism at their institutions (Brint and Karabel, 1989), there have been major changes in the area of vocational education that reflect the demands of industry.

In the 1980s, enrollment in general education classes increased, while vocational education (with the exception of business education) was either stagnant or decreasing. Moreover, according to Goodwin (1989), the number of students who actually completed specifically designed vocational programs dropped considerably. These enrollment changes reflect an important debate over the role and function of vocational education within the community college. Two-year vocational education programs were originally intended to prepare young people just out of high school for entry-level jobs in a particular field. These programs were developed within American secondary institutions and then extended into community colleges and technical schools. Normally, vocational education was delivered in tightly structured sets of courses that taught skills related to one particular occupation. Classes were taught by instructors who had industrial experience. The assumption was that if a program taught an individual the skills associated with a particular occupation, that individual would find a job.

As discussed in the preceding section, this traditional model is increasingly inappropriate for community college programs. First, many of the students in these programs already have entry-level jobs and are looking for skills that will advance them on their career paths. Second, while the programs tend to emphasize hands-on learning, employers are demanding more basic literacy and critical thinking skills. Third, because these are tightly structured sets of courses, vocational education students are often separated from the rest of the campus community, reinforcing the image of vocational education as a remedial area for students who cannot make the grade in general education and the sciences. Finally, because most of these programs do not include specific placement activities for their students, they do not even find them entry-level work.

For these reasons, there is a compelling need to move vocational education away from the overemphasis on hands-on skills in order to develop programs that meet the needs of employers. In 1990, the Michigan Board of Education appointed a fifty-person committee to develop a strategic plan for vocational education. The committee rejected the notion that vocational education simply involves the preparation of individuals in the area of technical skills. The statement of the group called for the elimination of "the artificial wall between academics and vocational courses and programs" (Michigan Board of Education, 1990, p. 2).

General Education and the World of Work

All of these changes suggest positive developments for the integration of general education and vocational education. However, these same changes in industry also mean that there must be a reformulation of how general education, as a subject matter and curriculum, can be made relevant to the world of work. The essence of this reformulation is simple: The generalizable skills taught in liberal arts courses are critical for the workers of the future. How is the subject matter of general education considered a critical skill? The use of computers in the world of work has changed the nature of

learning. As Berryman (1990, p. 7) has argued, "The most profound education implication of computers in the workplace is that they force a replacement of *observational learning* with *learning acquired primarily through
symbols,* whether verbal or mathematical." This second kind of learning concerns the ability to learn, the ability to relate, the ability to reason, and the
ability to communicate—all skills that are found within the general education curriculum. There is an additional dimension to the issue of critical
skills that has less to do with the skills necessary to perform a particular task
than with the shifting nature of careers, work, and firm enterprise. The
American economy is becoming dominated by firms that are subject to extraordinary flexibility and change. In the past, an individual could depend
on job stability in a particular industry; however, career disruptions and job
changes are becoming increasingly commonplace. The average adult may
change careers three to four times during a working lifetime. Thus, programs that offer both specific training in skills for particular jobs as well as
general education skills pertinent to career moves are well-suited for the
current employment climate.

The development of courses and the teaching processes for the integration of vocational education and general education will necessarily be different from the present, separate approaches of each field. To initiate the
required changes, instructors from both backgrounds must meet collectively
and develop a unified means by which their perspectives can be organized
into a program, thereby ending the traditional fragmentation of the courses.
This program would combine the abstract concepts of general education
and the specific technical skills that must be mastered in a particular vocational area. For example, reading skills could be taught through mastery of
job-related material. Both sides should attempt to find a common means by
which students can demonstrate competence of learning objectives. Indeed,
both general education instructors and vocational educators can start with
the same material—the concrete conditions of work—and proceed with
their themes and conceptions based on these specific conditions. This is not
simply a utopian call for more communication between disciplines. Rather,
the call is for a restructuring of teaching concepts around the demands of
the work situation.

It may be useful, and perhaps necessary, for the instructors to gain first-
hand experience from the workplace so that the subject matter linkages can
be more easily made. Clearly, learning in the work world is based far more
on collective doing than on individual mastery of skills. This may mean an
approach that emphasizes contextual understanding of the concepts and issues raised in the general education courses.

All of the above recommendations for the integration of general and vocational education may clash with the traditional culture of the general education professor who individually decides on the text and uses the classroom
discussion to amplify and "bring-out" particular topics of his or her own

choosing. However, just as industry has learned to become flexible and to market products designed for specific niches, so too must the education system develop a flexibility and a willingness to respond to the needs of its clients. If it is true, as has been argued here, that general education is relevant to the work force, then it is incumbent on general education instructors to learn how to reach their clients through effective teaching methods.

Unfortunately, there is no guarantee that a client-sensitive integration of academic and vocational instruction will naturally emerge out of the concern for the education and training of the future work force. Indeed, what appears to be in the forecast is more of a "shotgun marriage" where, in answer to the call from the business community for more basic skills, vocational educators simply add more hours for general education.

The expected outcome of an increase in general education hours taught, without any major structural changes, is more segmentation of learning and less understanding by workers of how the academic and vocational areas of knowledge interrelate. Attempts will be made to offer watered-down versions of general education, where only technical writing as opposed to composition is taught, or where "shop math" instead of principles is developed. Thus, despite the needs of business for learning skills taught within the general education arena, the attempt to introduce "more" may well result in "less." What is required is a true marriage that meets the needs of both partners, general and vocational education.

References

Arnsdorf, D., and Jacobs, J. "The Design and Management of CAD Systems in Post-Secondary Education and Training Programs." *Journal of Engineering and Computer Applications,* 1990, 4, 52–56.

Berryman, S. E. *Skills, Schools, and Signals.* Institute on Education and the Economy Occasional Papers, no. 2. New York: Institute on Education and the Economy, 1990. 24 pp. (ED 327 591)

Brint, S., and Karabel, J. *The Diverted Dream: Community Colleges and the Promise of Educational Opportunity in America, 1900–1985.* New York: Oxford University Press, 1989.

Carnevale, A. P., and Gainer, L. J. *The Learning Enterprise.* Alexandria, Va.: American Society for Training and Development, 1989. 61 pp. (ED 304 581)

Chisman, F. P. *Jump Start: The Federal Rule in Adult Literacy.* Southport, Conn.: Southport Institute, 1989. 47 pp. (ED 302 675)

Committee for Economic Development. *Investing in Our Children: Business and the Public Schools.* New York: Committee for Economic Development, 1985. 134 pp. (ED 261 117)

DePietro, R., and others. *Post-Secondary Vocational Education in a Technological Economy: Defining the Quality of Programs.* Ann Arbor, Mich.: Industrial Technology Institute, 1989.

Goodwin, D. *Postsecondary Vocational Education: National Assessment of Vocational Education Final Report.* Vol. 4. Washington, D.C.: National Assessment of Vocational Education, 1989. 148 pp. (ED 317 661)

Illinois Community College Board. *Fiscal Year 1987 Economic Development Grants Annual Report.* Springfield: Illinois Community College Board, 1987.

Jacobs, J. *The Extent of Customizing Training in Michigan Community Colleges.* Ann Arbor, Mich.: Industrial Technical Institute, 1989.

Jacobs, J., and McAlinden, S. P. *The Impact of Programmable Automation on Employee Training and Occupational Change in American Manufacturing*. Ann Arbor, Mich.: Industrial Technology Institute, 1991.

Kazis, R. "The Relationship Between Education and Productivity: Implications for the Competitiveness of American Manufacturing and the Movement for Educational Reform." Unpublished manuscript, Department of Political Science, Massachusetts Institute of Technology, 1988.

McAlinden, S. P. *Programmable Automation, Labor Productivity, and the Competitiveness of Midwestern Manufacturing*. Ann Arbor, Mich.: Industrial Technology Institute, 1989.

Majchrzak, A. *Education and Training for CAD/CAM: Results of a National Probability Survey*. Krannert Institute Paper Series. West Lafayette, Ind.: Purdue University, 1985. 32 pp. (ED 263 941)

Mehrens, W. *Michigan Employability Skills Technical Report*. Lansing: Michigan Department of Education, 1989.

Michigan Board of Education. *Strategic Plan for Vocational Technical Education in Michigan*. Lansing: Michigan Board of Education, 1990.

Phelps, L. A., Brandenburg, D. C., and Jacobs, J. *The UAW Joint Funds: Opportunities and Dilemmas for Post-Secondary Education*. Berkeley, Calif.: National Center for Research in Vocational Education, 1990. 45 pp. (ED 328 765)

Piore, M. J., and Sabel, C. F. *The Second Industrial Divide*. New York: Basic Books, 1984.

JAMES JACOBS is director of policy research at Macomb County Community College, Warren, Michigan, and former senior researcher for the Industrial Technology Institute, Ann Arbor.

*Humanities and technical-professional educators have artificially separated
general education and vocational education to the disadvantage of students.
This chapter recommends ways to take down those barriers.*

General Education in Occupational
Programs: The Barriers
Can Be Surmounted

Carole Finley Edmonds

There appears to be general consensus that students in occupational programs need more than concrete skills to perform well in the work force
(American Association of Community and Junior Colleges, 1988a, 1988b;
Cheney, 1986). What these students need is general education. But as faculty and as administrators with diverse approaches and considerations, we
have not yet found a mutually acceptable definition of general education.
Thus, we need, first, to reach a consensus on what constitutes general education. Then, our task is to negotiate ways to change what we are currently
doing in order to provide an integrated approach to teaching and measuring
essential job skills. This integration of general and occupational education is
necessary if we are to ensure that the learning experience truly prepares students for the workplace.

The issue for the 1990s is not whether educators from liberal arts disciplines and occupational studies can agree with each other and with employers on who should drive the cart that we know as general education. By and
large, curricula will remain the responsibility of administrators and faculty
in the colleges, and hiring and promotion will remain the responsibility of
employers. The challenge is to integrate occupational programs and general
education so that students see the connectedness of their learning, practice
problem solving, work cooperatively with others, and construct and evaluate alternatives. Furthermore, these outcomes must be measured in imagina-
tive and substantive ways.

NEW DIRECTIONS FOR COMMUNITY COLLEGES, no. 81, Spring 1993 © Jossey-Bass Publishers

The Problem of Barriers Between General and Occupational Education

The obstacles to the goals articulated above lie primarily within the academy. On this point, the experience of the Shared Vision Task Force, a group of six members of the National Council for Occupational Education and six members of the Community College Humanities Association, is illustrative. In 1986, as they began the task of improving the quality of occupational programs in community and junior colleges across the nation through the integration of a humanities component, they discovered that the surface of the water looks calm but there is much turbulence underneath. While, publicly, occupationally focused educators and educators in the liberal arts and general education appear to get along, there are deep divisions that will have to be crossed if the needs of students are to be met.

Language is the means that we must use to come together, but as the Shared Vision Task Force found in a number of fiery meetings, language also reflects the difficulties that we have to overcome. The Shared Vision Task Force was created to study and offer recommendations on how to bring the humanities component into occupational programs. The integration of a humanities component was viewed as a more difficult task than that of bringing in writing or mathematics since components of these disciplines were already present in occupational programs. Their vital role in the preparation of students for employment has long been recognized. But the role and value of the humanities remains to be established.

The members of the Shared Vision Task Force included individuals who had helped write *Humanities Policy Statement* (American Association of Community and Junior Colleges, 1986) and *Criteria for Excellence in Associate in Applied Science Degree Programs* (American Association of Community and Junior Colleges, 1985), seemingly ensuring that the language of these documents would be understood among the task force members and would inform their "shared vision." But the reality proved otherwise. Turbulence that is often conveniently and politely buried by separate curricula and separate faculty at comprehensive community colleges and by like-minded faculty at technical and junior colleges surfaced. Portions of the *Humanities Policy Statement* text, such as "study of the humanities encourages the best habits of the mind" (American Association of Community and Junior Colleges, 1986, p. 1), seemed infuriatingly "fuzzy" to the occupational educators on the task force. Humanities educators fumed at the "outcomes orientation," that is, measurable learning outcomes as essential to "all components of (the occupational) degree, including general education," stressed in *Criteria for Excellence in Associate in Applied Science Degree Programs*. Beyond these language (and values) differences loomed major differences in what constitutes "real" education, "mere" training, essential learning, frills, and college-level coursework.

Faculty members' and administrators' resistance to change is not formally acknowledged with these value-laden words. Instead, certain reasoned arguments representative of the hidden disagreements throughout our community, technical and junior colleges come forward, revealing linguistic chasms among interest groups that need to be bridged. For group members, the label "real education" applies only to the activities of their own group. "Frills," "fuzzy-headed," and "academic" (used pejoratively) categorize the liberal arts to occupational educators. For liberal arts educators, "training" (as a negative term designating what is not real education), "skills," and "terminal" still categorize the occupational curricula. The need of students in occupational programs for a balanced, integrated curriculum—one that provides specific skills as well as the attitudes and understandings essential to handle change, work with others, and see alternatives—is ignored or glossed over with a "we cover that" or a "we offer those courses."

The occupational educators usually jump quickly to two points. First, they state that their respective curricula are already too full with over seventy required semester hours, a figure that is significantly above the sixty to sixty-two semester hours required for an associate degree. Each course is considered essential to all students. Second, their advisory committees, state licensing examinations, and standards of patient, product, or client safety mandate the curricula, although they say that more general education components, in particular, humanities, would be "nice." These discussions end, too often, with a statement similar to "we will put them on an optional electives list."

Both arguments dealing with course requirements have validity to a degree; however, they fail to address the issue of what students will need on the job. Studies show that most job dismissals and poor performance ratings center on employees' poor attitudes, poor interaction with others, or inability to deal with change (American Association of Community and Junior Colleges, 1988b). The advisory committee argument is difficult to refute at first glance because these groups are, after all, made up of professionals in the particular field served by an occupational program. The problem, however, is that these practitioners may be influenced by a lack of general education in their own preparation. Furthermore, their attitudes have been affected by a failure of program directors to ask the right questions about essential employee behaviors, understandings, and attitudes. There is also a bias toward saying that the program already provides skills in working with others through intern or cooperative education experiences.

Occupational educators may also have negative responses to the integration of additional general education components, particularly those in the humanities, into occupational programs because of their personal experiences in general education as undergraduates, including their own associate degree courses at community colleges. They probably were enrolled in general education courses, particularly in humanities, social science, and science, that were aimed at providing a foundation for literature or sociology or chemistry majors rather than providing general education needed by all associate degree graduates regardless of occupation.

The split between occupational and general education faculty and administrators too often results in both groups feeling attacked. The issue of relevance sidetracked the real issue when general education courses came under fire in the 1970s. The argument of the students seemed initially to be about currency, while the argument among faculty was almost always about content—office information systems or nursing content versus history content or literature content. While what is taught matters, the in- and out-of-class activities in which students are asked to engage and the way in which learning is measured clearly matter greatly, particularly in view of what employers expect of their employees. While the history of some nursing practices may be taught in a nursing program, the overall significance of historiography or values in a particular society as a way of understanding health care and health practitioners is seldom taught. Courses on measurement, if taught, seldom ask students to deal with primary source material and draw conclusions about what has happened or is happening. Still less frequent is the practice of asking students to work collaboratively to reflect on these sources using the techniques of historians and to draw mutually agreed-on conclusions. Too often what is supposed to be general education is merely rote memorization, recited on examinations.

General education must be integrated into occupational programs. It needs to be revised extensively to focus on an understanding of ways of knowing used by historians, literary theorists, and biologists, for example, and on the methodological practices of those fields, which are then evaluated using appropriate content measurements. Liberal arts education is not perfect either. It needs to expand its focus on integrating knowledge through process.

At Southern Maine Technical College, humanities and occupational faculty have worked together to integrate humanities into occupational programs. With strong administrative support, the English, law enforcement, and allied health and radiology departments redefined the mission of a technical college from training and service to industry to a more complex statement addressing general education. The committee started by revising an American literature course to include "examination of insights and reflections that contribute to the heterogeneity of American society" and examination of "the connection between the study of literature and the demands of the workplace" (Southern Maine Technical College, 1989, p. 1). Program implementation also began in law enforcement and radiography, where objectives in Introduction to Law Enforcement, Management of Police Forces, and Introduction to Health Services were revised to mirror objectives in the literature course. When the literature course talked about race, law enforcement officers spoke to the class. Humanities and occupational faculty made a combined effort to ensure, as one teacher put it, that there was no "wink-and-blink" commitment to the inclusion of humanities. Students have been enthusiastic not only about the literature course and the linkages to their occupational courses but also about a course on ethical dilemmas. Faculty report that students are "selling the courses" to other students. The students see the connections between the complex social issues addressed in the ethics class and the problems and decisions that will face them in the work world.

Change such as that taking place at Southern Maine is not easy. Attitudes must change if the curriculum is to advance in significant ways. Multiple approaches to materials selection, classroom activities, assignments, and assessment are needed to meet the needs of diverse occupational programs and student populations. Most important, the Southern Maine experience shows instruction must foster much more integration of learning.

The distribution requirement approach to general education in all types of higher education has been questioned extensively for failing to give students an integrated picture of the way various disciplines interrelate and view the same issues (Boyer, 1987; Gaff, 1983). Community college demographics indicate that these students may need more help integrating learning than is needed by their four-year university and college peers. Their backgrounds usually include fewer college preparatory classes in the sciences and humanities because many of them never planned to go to college. They are older than traditional college students, and they have already made many adult decisions and become economically independent without these courses. Many are first-generation college students. They do not assume that learning to change their attitudes and behaviors significantly is a purpose for attending college. Rather, they enroll to learn the ways of knowing and doing in particular occupations.

Still, change is possible and can begin with classic texts as well as examination of the objectives in occupational programs. For instance, the efforts of the Advancing the Humanities Project of the American Association of Community and Junior Colleges led to faculty study in preparation for a new integrative humanities course at Kalamazoo Valley Community College in Michigan. A summer seminar for technology, science, and humanities faculty, funded by the National Endowment for the Humanities, addressed such traditional texts as Dante's *Inferno*.

Over a two-year period, 1991–1993, two summer seminars and colloquia during the academic years following the summer institutes have led to a new general education core course: The Humanities, Science and Technology: Making Connections. In addition to Dante, faculty studied major thinkers such as Aristotle, Plato, and Darwin with the help of visiting scholars. Throughout, the focus was on making connections. For instance, Robert Sessions, professor of philosophy at Kirkwood Community College, Cedar Rapids, Iowa, focused on texts that deal with work, described in the project proposal as "the place where science and technology meet."

In the new core course, first offered in spring 1993, faculty from English, philosophy, humanities, automotive, drafting, physics, biology, and political science are helping teach the course, which is facilitated by a philosophy instructor. Faculty from other areas as diverse as nursing and music are lending support as visitors to the course. Throughout the course, students are exploring primary texts such as those read by faculty in the summer seminars to examine open-ended questions.

Finding a Solution: The Task Force Report

The Southern Maine Technical College and Kalamazoo Valley Community College programs exemplify different ways of implementing a shared vision. Discussion among educators, which can lead to agreement on language and on goals, also holds promise, as the Shared Vision Task Force's final report (American Association of Community and Junior Colleges, 1988b) has shown. The report indicated ten unique and significant contributions of humanities in occupational programs. It also outlined recommendations for the revision progress. During the period 1989–1990, five model site projects attempted to implement the recommendations. Each used humanities and occupational faculty to develop a different approach to integrating a humanities component. On each campus, barriers of attitude, often reflected in language, had to be overcome.

Nevertheless, the development projects at the model sites and the task force's efforts to measure whether the new humanities components changed students' thinking and attitudes have resulted in cooperation among occupational and humanities faculty. They also resulted in an integration of considerations from the work world into humanities instruction, and of humanities into occupational courses.

An office technology instructor and humanities instructor are team-teaching a new course called Changes and Choices at Eastern Iowa Community College, one of the model program sites. They have developed their own text—an edited collection ranging from "Demosthenes Denounces Philip of Macedon" to Tillie Olson's "As I Stand Ironing," to Martin Luther King, Jr.'s "Letter from a Birmingham Jail"—which considers how change comes into human experience and how choices can be made. Students study and hear about the contributions of the humanities to the work world as the readings on workplace issues are interwoven with literature and philosophy.

King and Bella (1987, p. 7) aptly describe the approach: "All concepts, theories and intellectual constructions, and all actions and behaviors, can be fully understood in their webs of relationships." Efforts of this kind require a willingness to trust one another, work together, and commit our time to provide our students with learning experiences that will prepare them for a technological society that demands the abilities to work with others, to adapt to change, and to consider alternatives. These efforts must occur across the country if we are to meet the needs of our students.

References

American Association of Community and Junior Colleges. *Criteria for Excellence in Associate in Applied Science Degree Programs.* National Council for Occupational Education Monograph Series, vol. 2, no. 1. Washington, D.C.: American Association of Community and Junior Colleges, 1985. 12 pp. (ED 278 430)

American Association of Community and Junior Colleges. *Humanities Policy Statement.* Washington, D.C.: American Association of Community and Junior Colleges, 1986.

American Association of Community and Junior Colleges. *Building Communities: A Vision for a New Century.* Report of the Commission on the Future of Community Colleges. Washington, D.C.: American Association of Community and Junior Colleges, 1988a. 58 pp. (ED 293 578)

American Association of Community and Junior Colleges. *Integrating the Humanities into Associate Degree Occupational Programs: Final Report of the Shared Vision Task Force.* Washington, D.C.: American Association of Community and Junior Colleges, 1988b. 76pp. (ED 305 093)

Boyer, E. L. *College: The Undergraduate Experience in America.* New York: Harper & Row, 1987.

Cheney, L. V. "Students of Success: A Liberal-Arts Training Is Increasingly Valuable in the American Corporation." *Newsweek,* Sept. 1, 1986, p. 7.

Gaff, J. G. *General Education Today: A Critical Analysis of Controversies, Practices, and Reforms.* San Francisco: Jossey-Bass, 1983.

Kalamazoo Valley Community College. "The Humanities, Science, and Technology: Making Connections." Unpublished proposal to the National Endowment for the Humanities, 1990.

King, J., and Bella, D. "Taking Context Seriously." *Liberal Education,* 1987, 73 (3), 7–13.

Southern Maine Technical College. *American Literature.* South Portland: Southern Maine Technical College, 1989.

CAROLE FINLEY EDMONDS *is dean of arts and sciences at Kellogg Community College, Battle Creek, Michigan.*

An annotated bibliography is provided on general education in community colleges, including general background on the topic and discussions of the relationship between general education and lifelong learning, the globalization of general education, and the role of general education in occupational and vocational programs.

Sources and Information: General Education in the Community College

Neal A. Raisman, Karin Petersen Hsiao

Since the series *New Directions for Community Colleges* last focused on general education (Johnson, 1982), numerous reports on the topic have appeared. National studies, focusing primarily on public school and university education, have increased the country's awareness of deficiencies in our education system and brought renewed vigor to the debate on general education. Moreover, works such as *The Closing of the American Mind* (Bloom, 1987), *Cultural Literacy: What Every American Needs to Know* (Hirsch, 1987), and *What Do Our 17-Year-Olds Know?* (Ravitch and Finn, 1987) have sparked a discussion in which participants frequently point to general education as a primary example of the failure of American education.

The review of general education has not abated in recent years. If anything, it has intensified as participants have moved from lists of what students know (Hirsch, 1987) or do not know (Ravitch and Finn, 1987) to broader indictments. Works such as *Prof-Scam: Professors and the Demise of Higher Education* (Sykes, 1988) and the more thoughtful, almost plaintive, *American Professors: A National Resource Imperiled* (Bowen and Schuster, 1986) express a belief that there are serious problems with postsecondary general education in a system that is built on research-based promotion.

Although, in the past, much of the debate focused on the university and the high school, thus omitting discussion of the status of general education at community and junior colleges, the literature on general education in the two-year institution has grown in recent years. The following sources represent the most current literature in the ERIC data base on general education in the community college. Most ERIC documents (references with ED numbers) can be read on microfiche at over eight hundred libraries world-wide. In addition, most may be ordered on microfiche or in paper copy from the ERIC Document Reproduction Service (EDRS) at (800) 443-ERIC. Journal articles are not available from EDRS, but they can be acquired through regular library channels or purchased from the University Microfilm International Articles Clearinghouse at (800) 521-0600, ext. 533.

General Articles

These sources present overviews of general education in the community college today, as well as recommendations for curriculum reform in the future.

Alabama State Commission on Higher Education. *Academic Preparation for College: What Students Need to Know and Be Able to Do to Enter College in Alabama.* Montgomery: Alabama State Commission on Higher Education, 1989. 28 pp. (ED 311 781)

This booklet outlines what college entrants need to know and be able to do to enter college in Alabama. As of July 1989, admissions standards of all Alabama public colleges and universities reflect the knowledge and skills described here: (1) basic academic competencies—reading, writing, speaking and listening, mathematics, reasoning, and studying and (2) basic academic subjects—English, the arts, mathematics, science, social studies, and foreign languages. Minimum requirements for the advanced academic diploma are also given.

Association of American Colleges. *A New Vitality in General Education: Planning, Teaching, and Supporting Effective Liberal Learning by the Task Group on General Education.* Washington, D.C.: Association of American Colleges, 1988. 64 pp. (ED 290 387) (Order from the Association of American Colleges, 1818 R Street, NW, Washington, DC 20009.)

As a central report that bears on community colleges as well as universities, this document begins by redefining general education and then describes the processes of rethinking and implementing new approaches, with examples from specific programs. The rationale, purposes, and scope of general education are considered, along with issues of implementation. Effective ways of planning programs and courses, teaching them, and supporting them are presented.

Bennett, W. J. *To Reclaim a Legacy: A Report on the Humanities in Higher Education.* Washington, D.C.: National Endowment for the Humanities, 1984. 63 pp. (ED 247 880)

Teaching and learning of the humanities at the baccalaureate level were assessed by a blue-ribbon study group of thirty-one nationally prominent authorities on higher education convened by the National Endowment for the Humanities. Attention was also given in the context of the humanities to how secondary and graduate education have affected undergraduate education and been affected by it. Answers were sought to three basic questions: (1) What is the condition of learning in the humanities? (2) Why is it as it is? (3) What, if anything, should be done about it? The report closes by identifying a set of specific questions that should be addressed by college presidents, humanities faculty, humanities departments, and the academic community in general.

Boyer, E. L. *College: The Undergraduate Experience in America.* New York: Harper & Row, 1987. (Order from HarperCollins, 10 East 53rd Street, New York, N.Y. 10022.)

The experience of baccalaureate-level students in the United States is considered with particular attention to the ways in which college structures and procedures affect students' lives. During fall 1984, site visits by sixteen observers-reporters were made to twenty-nine colleges and universities. National surveys of 5,000 faculty members and 4,500 undergraduates were also undertaken to obtain information about faculty and students: their age, sex, ethnicity, academic achievement, and views about teaching and learning. The status of general education was examined through a survey of 1,310 chief academic officers.

Cheney, L. V. *50 Hours: A Core Curriculum for College Students.* Washington, D.C.: National Endowment for the Humanities, 1989. 116 pp. (ED 308 804)

Information for colleges engaged in curriculum reform about how other schools are managing the task is presented, the central device for organizing details being an imagined core of studies—fifty semester hours—that encourages coherent and substantive learning in essential areas of knowledge. Rather than acting as a single prototype, this report provides information about various models to individual faculties who must decide the undergraduate course of study.

Cohen, A. M. "What Can Be Done About General Education?" Paper presented at a conference of the Liberal Arts Network for Development, East Lansing, Michigan, January 26–27, 1989. 17 pp. (ED 307 014)

The idea of general education has ebbed and flowed for generations. Recent calls for general education, appearing both in the professional and popular literature, demand an integrative curriculum that brings people toward common understandings. The content of what is taught matters less than the need for a continuous effort to enhance social cohesion and move students toward a realization that participation in the polity is important. Since the community college curriculum centers on the liberal arts and occupational studies, general education must be diffused throughout these areas. Integrated, self-contained, interdisciplinary general education courses should be required for every student in the institution, and their outcomes assessed globally, in order to bring a greater understanding of the broader society and of the student's place within it.

Cronk, G. *General Education Reform in the New Jersey Community Colleges: The Bergen Community College Experience, 1982–1987.* Princeton, N.J.: Mid-Career Fellowship Program, Princeton University, 1988. 47 pp. (ED 297 789)

An overview is provided of the development of Bergen Community College's (BCC) general education curriculum between 1982 and 1987. Introductory comments review the state regulations implemented in 1983 to govern general education at all New Jersey community colleges. Next, Cronk explains the original charge and final recommendations of BCC's Committee on General Education, which resulted in the revision of all BCC degree and certificate programs in accordance with a new system of general education requirements. The author then discusses the organization of the current program. Finally, he summarizes major changes in the general education program and considers the effects of the curriculum changes on enrollment and registration patterns. Unresolved problems and concerns are identified.

Education Commission of the States. Task Force on Education for Economic Growth. *Action for Excellence: A Comprehensive Plan to Improve Our Nation's Schools.* Denver, Colo.: Education Commission of the States, 1983. 60 pp. (ED 235 588)

Following an argument for improving the quality of public education to further the nation's economic growth, current educational deficiencies are analyzed and an action plan presented. Methods for implementing the recommendations are outlined. Various encouraging signs of success are cited in terms of achieving both a higher quality of education for all and greater equality of educational opportunity. A list of redefined and upgraded basic skills and competencies for productive employment is appended.

Greenfield, R. K. "Continuation of the Community College Vigor: Strengthening the Liberal Arts, General Education, and Transfer Education." In J. Eaton (ed.), *Colleges of Choice.* New York: American Council on Education/Macmillan, 1988.

Greenfield places general education and the liberal arts within the context of collegiate mission, priorities, access, excellence, and comprehensiveness and discusses how to make general education a central component of each of these aspects of collegiate mandate. The transfer function is seen as a major element of collegiate identity and a central component of a redefined focus for general education, which needs a workable definition to set curriculum and program features in place. Change is needed to reinvigorate the general education component and the comprehensive mission.

Johnson County Community College. *Creating an Alternative General Education Core Curriculum.* Overland Park, Kans.: Johnson County Community College, 1989. 27 pp. (ED 307 006)

A description is provided of Johnson County Community College's (JCCC) efforts to reform its general education curriculum. An introductory section notes the objectives of the nationwide reform movement and discusses the college's replacement of a free elective system with distribution requirements, the development of the "Aims of General Education" statement to guide curriculum development, and the initial steps taken to create a core curriculum. The next section traces the deliberations of the General Education Subcommittee over what form of core to specify and presents the subcommittee's recommendations concerning a nonmandated core curriculum. Next, the collaborative process used in course development is explained, and the resulting core curriculum is presented. The final section underscores the status of the core curriculum as an alternative to, rather than a replacement for, the distribution elective requirements and reviews the aims of general education at JCCC.

Klein, T., and Gaff, J. G. *Reforming General Education : A Survey.* Washington, D.C.: Center for General Education, Association of American Colleges, 1982. (Order from the Association of American Colleges, 1818 R Street, NW, Washington, DC 20009.)

The authors report on a survey of the nature of program changes taking place in undergraduate general education and factors that affect curriculum change. A sample of 272 colleges and universities that were conducting serious review or revision of their undergraduate general education programs were sent questionnaires; 139 responses were received. Attitudes toward general education at 71 percent of the schools had become more favorable during the three-year period prior to the survey. Eighty-two institutions had adopted a curriculum revision or had a specific proposal before the faculty. Requirements in the humanities, arts, natural sciences, and social sciences had been increased in 32 to 52 percent of the institutions. Skills that received explicit attention were writing (99 percent of the programs), mathematics (82 percent), critical thinking (79 percent), and problem solving (72 percent). There were qualitative changes in integration, global studies, a four-year course of study, and nonlecture pedagogy.

Raisman, N. A. "Creating Philosopher-Bricklayers: Redefining General Education and the Liberal Arts." *Community, Technical, and Junior College Journal,* 1991–1992, *62* (3), 16–20.

The question of whether community colleges are providing valid liberal arts and general education curricula is considered from the standpoints of community college critics and supporters. An argument is made for a definition of liberal arts and general education that takes into account the educational aspirations of community college students. Raisman considers the fine line between liberal and general education.

Vaughan, G. B. "General Education: The Community College's Unfulfilled Agenda." Paper prepared for the conference General Studies: Continuing Issues and Emerging Prospects, Nelsonville, Ohio, April 17, 1989. 22 pp. (ED 305 966)

   Community colleges have always embraced general education in principle but have largely failed to deliver a meaningful program of general studies. Possible reasons for that failure, and steps that can be taken to develop a meaningful program of general education, are presented.

General Education and Lifelong Learning

General Education provides an opportunity for community colleges to teach overall competence and thinking skills that will be of value to students throughout their lives.

Englehardt, E. E. "A Core Approach to Teaching Ethics." *Community, Technical, and Junior College Journal,* 1991–1992, *62* (3), 30–34.

   This article describes Utah Valley Community College's core course Ethics and Values, which approaches timely and interdisciplinary topics (for example, abortion and business ethics) and emphasizes writing, self-confrontation, oral discussion, and critical thinking. Problems in promoting active student learning are discussed, along with the use of collaborative learning and other approaches.

Harlacher, E. L. "Community General Education." In B. L. Johnson (ed.), *General Education in Two-Year Colleges.* New Directions for Community Colleges, no. 40. San Francisco: Jossey-Bass, 1982.

   Community general education provides a unique opportunity for community colleges to enhance the overall quality of community life, prepare citizens for their responsibilities in a democracy, and help them participate creatively in life activities. This chapter cites examples of innovative and effective community general education programs.

Higginbottom, G. H. *The Civic Ground of Collegiate General Education and the Community College.* Working Paper Series No. 1-91. Binghamton, N.Y.: Institute for Community College Research, Broome Community College, 1991. 107 pp. (ED 338 277)

   The two chapters of this book offer a rationale for the inclusion of civic education as a nexus of community college general education. The first chapter provides an introductory overview of various issues related to general education reform and the new emphasis among educators and critics on postsecondary civic or citizenship education. The second chapter reviews the history of community college general and civic education from the institution's beginnings and provides a critical discussion of the civic education commitments of selected community college general education plans connected with the curriculum reforms of the 1980s. It concludes with a model of community college general and civic education that incorporates a generic collegiate design but is responsible to the unique circumstances of the two-year college.

Miles, C. *Disciplinary Versus General Competence: Coming Curricular Revolution? The Example of Teaching Thinking.* Southern Association of Community and Junior Colleges and Technical Colleges Occasional Paper, vol. 7, no. 1. Greenwood, S.C.: Southern Association of Community and Junior Colleges and Technical Colleges, 1989. 6 pp. (ED 311 950)

Increasing numbers of students neither enter nor leave the education system with the competencies necessary for effective performance as workers, students, family members, and citizens. The solution to this problem lies with integration of content and general instruction, and with emphasis on thinking skills across the curriculum. Rather than memorizing or ignoring complex problems, students trained in critical thinking reflect, explore, examine, discuss, and defend their insights and mental processes. Students with the ability to think critically will meet the growing demand for competent communicators, thinkers, and learners.

Saunders, W. S. "Education for Interpersonal Life." *Liberal Education,* 1990, 76 (2), 11–13.

Higher education does not address the central challenges of daily interpersonal life—parenting, marriage, friendships, child rearing, and dealing with change, loss, sickness, and death. But education can instill "tacit knowing," that is, knowing in the bones, prior to conceptualization or verbalization. This knowing can be imparted by great literature.

Wiggins, G. "The Futility of Trying to Teach Everything of Importance." *Educational Leadership,* 1989, 47 (3), 44–48.

The problem of student learning is really about adult ignorance of how to achieve thoughtful and long-lasting understanding. Conventional curricula reinforce the idea that knowledge is uncontroversial and self-evident, whereas the modern educational task is to put students in the habit of thoughtful inquiry.

The Globalization of General Education

The incorporation of international studies into the general education curriculum will increase its relevance to today's students.

Fersh, S. H. "Adding an International Dimension to the Community College: Examples and Implications." In R. K. Greenfield (ed.), *Developing International Education Programs*. New Directions for Community Colleges, no. 70. San Francisco: Jossey-Bass, 1990.

This chapter describes nine community colleges with strong international programs and identifies resources to help administrators interested in initiating international education programs. The value of an international component in general education to help individuals transcend cultural conditioning is stressed.

Glock, N. C. "Rethinking the Curriculum to Meet the Needs of Underprepared, Underrepresented, and Economically Disadvantaged Students: Majors and Courses for the 21st Century." Paper presented at the annual conference Ethnic and Language Minorities, Sacramento, California, February 28–March 2, 1990. 12 pp. (ED 319 467)

General education offerings should be restructured to give students the skills and resources needed to make sense out of their particular gender and ethnicity, while emphasizing not the old world or new world but rather the one world shared by students and teachers. The resulting core curriculum would be (1) socially cohesive, providing common reference points to all members of society; (2) culturally inclusive, drawing on diverse human cultures and affirming the contributions of all social classes; (3) ethically selective, supporting values necessary to environmental and species survival and human fulfillment; (4) conceptually generative, providing skills and general principles that allow for the synthesis and critical assessment of information; and (5) personally significant, creating options for in-depth study of particular cultures, classes, and conditions.

McNamara, L. L. *Internationalizing the Curriculum: One Instructor's Experience*. Orlando, Fla.: Valencia Community College, 1990. 10 pp. (ED 316 294)

Using a Title VI grant from the U.S. Department of Education, McNamara, a faculty member at Valencia Community College, developed international or intercultural modules for existing courses to explore both Western and non-Western contributions to the humanities. In this book, she describes several modules developed during the first two years of the grant.

Spain, L. "The Image of the Other: Media Support for a Pluralistic Curriculum." Paper presented at the 10th annual meeting of the Community College General Education Association, New York, November 2–3, 1989. 8 pp. (ED 311 972)

The integration of pluralism into the general education curriculum has long been a goal of the community college. The audiovisual resources of the college library can be particularly useful in examining and exploring other cultures, and in breaking down the barriers between members of one culture and "the other," that is, those on the other side of the artificial walls based on differences in race, sex, cultural background, age, and sexual preference. Examples of audiovisual materials that document negative and stereotypical images of "the other" are provided. A selected bibliography of films and videotapes related to the promotion of pluralism is appended.

Thomas, T. R. *Integrated Humanities: A Participatory Course for a Multi-Cultural Environment.* Los Alamos, N.M.: Center for Nonlinear Studies, Los Alamos National Laboratory, 1991. 23 pp. (ED 332 735)

A course description and syllabus are provided for Integrated Humanities, a general education course taught at Northern New Mexico Community College to provide students with a solid, reliable knowledge base and framework within which to pursue educational experiences. The course syllabus provides descriptions of thirty week-long units structured around academic lectures and related activities designed to illustrate the relationship between the lectures and actual life experiences. Each unit description includes ten vocabulary terms for students, and suggestions and explanations for the instructor.

General Education and Vocational and Occupational Programs

General education can and should play an important role in community college occupational and vocational programs.

Armistead, L. P., Lemon, J., Perkins, D. R., and Armistead, J. S. "The Amount and Importance of General Education in the Two-Year Occupational Curriculum According to Corporate Employers." *Community/Junior College Quarterly of Research and Practice,* 1989, *13* (2), 91–99.

The authors describe a survey of two hundred corporate employers regarding the proportion of the vocational curriculum that should be devoted to general education. Over half (52 percent) of the responding employers felt that general education should comprise approximately 30 percent of the vocational curriculum, and that communication, critical thinking, and employability skills should also be emphasized.

Nolte, W. H. "Guaranteed Student Success: General Education and Occupational Programs." *Community College Review,* 1991, *19* (1), 14–23.

Nolte defines issues and options related to general education in two-year college occupational programs and discusses why students, employers, and society need general education. Minimum general education requirements proposed by various organizations are reviewed, as well as particular competencies to be developed; Nolte also discusses ways to achieve general education in occupational programs.

Sessions, R. "Humanities and Career Education: Bridging the Great Divide." *Community, Technical, and Junior College Journal,* 1991–1992, *62* (3), 35–37.

Kirkwood Community College has attempted to bridge the division between its humanities and vocational programs through a one-course humanities requirement for associate of applied science students. This article describes the development of three humanities courses by humanities and vocational faculty, citing the rationale for development of the courses and reviewing results, including improved faculty cooperation and appreciation.

References

Bloom, A. D. *The Closing of the American Mind.* New York: Simon & Schuster, 1987.

Bowen, H. R., and Schuster, J. H. *American Professors: A National Resource Imperiled.* New York: Oxford University Press, 1986.

Hirsch, E. D. *Cultural Literacy: What Every American Needs to Know.* Boston: Houghton Mifflin, 1987.

Johnson, B. L. (ed.). *General Education in Two-Year Colleges.* New Directions for Community Colleges, no. 40. San Francisco: Jossey-Bass, 1982.

Ravitch, D., and Finn, C. E., Jr. *What Do Our 17-Year-Olds Know?: A Report on the First National Assessment of History and Literature.* New York: Harper & Row, 1987.

Sykes, C. J. *Profscam: Professors and the Demise of Higher Education.* New York: Kampmann, 1988.

NEAL A. RAISMAN is associate provost and special assistant for university planning at the University of Cincinnati,Cincinnati, Ohio.

KARIN PETERSEN HSIAO is a former user services coordinator at the ERIC Clearinghouse for Junior Colleges, University of California, Los Angeles.

INDEX

Access, and quality, 9
Adelman, C., 23
Administrators, and general education, 19
Advancing the Humanities Project, 89
Aesthetic values, 42
Alabama State Commission on Higher Education, 94
Alexander, P. A., 32
American Association of Community and Junior Colleges, 59, 85, 86, 87, 89, 90
American Council on Education, 1
American Professors: A National Resource Imperiled (Bowen and Schuster), 93
Anandam, K., 69
Applebee, A. N., 60
Armistead, J. S., 101
Armistead, L. P., 101
Arnsdorf, D., 83
Assessment: and expert learner findings, 38; of students' values, 49–50
Association of American Colleges, 5, 10, 21, 22, 28, 29, 94
At-risk students, at University of Texas, 36. *See also* Minorities

Barrows, T. S., 54
Basic skills, 78–79
Bella, D., 90
Bennett, W. J., 94
Bergen Community College, 96
Bernstein, A., 10
Berryman, S. E., 82
Black, M., 60
Blake, H., 10
Bloom, A. D., 93
Bowen, H. R., 93
Boyer, E. L., 22, 67, 68, 69, 70, 71, 89, 95
Brandenburg, D. C., 78
Brawer, F. B., 14, 22, 23
Brint, S., 1, 80
Brown, M. H., 62
Business, skill needs of, 75–76. *See also* Vocational education; Workplace

Campbell, D. F., 64
Carl D. Perkins Vocational and Applied Technology Act, 75

Carnevale, A. P., 31, 77
Carter, D. J., 53
Cedar Valley College, 69
Center for the Study of Community Colleges (CSCC), 14, 16–17, 18
Cheney, L. V., 52, 85, 95
Chi, M.T.H., 31, 32
Chisman, F. P., 78
City University of New York, Queens College of, 71
Cleveland, H., 7
Closing of the American Mind, The (Bloom), 93
Clowes, D. A., 1, 70
Cognitive Learning Strategies Project, 36
Cognitive processes, development of, 35–36
Cohen, A. M., 14, 18, 22, 23, 95
Committee for Economic Development, 79
Communication, shared, 68–69
Community College Goals Inventory (CCGI) study, 13, 19
Community College Humanities Association, 86
Community colleges: general education at, 1, 21–24; and habits of thought, 27–29; occupational education at, 26–27; reform role of, 9–11; trends in, 6–7
Comprehension monitoring, by expert learners, 33–34
Computers: and learning for workplace, 82; study of, 69
Cranson, K. R., 62
Critical thinking skills, 78
Cronk, G., 96
Cross, K. P., 13, 14, 19
Cultural diffusion, 55
Cultural literacy, 52
Cultural Literacy: What Every American Needs to Know (Hirsch), 93
Curriculum: debate about, 5–6; globalized general education, 7, 54–58, 99–101; for minorities, 68–72; pluralistic, 100–101; proposal for general education, 67–68; trends in, 6–7; Western-grounded, 52–54. *See also* Metacurriculum

103

Customized training courses, 77
Cuyahoga Community College, 69

Dashiell, M., 61, 62
Delineated options approach, 45, 49–50
DePietro, R., 79
Developmental education: applications combining general and, 61–63; definition and antecedents of, 59–60; related to general education, 63–65
Durham Technical Community College, 68

Eastern Iowa Community College, 90
Eaton, J. S., 2, 21, 30
Economic values, 43
Edgerton, R., 8
Edmonds, C., 3, 85, 91
Education. *See* Developmental education; General education; Occupational education; Vocational education
Education Commission of the States, 96
Eheney, L. V., 71
El-Khawas, E. H., 53
Englehardt, E. E., 98
English, 59–60. *See also* Humanities
ERIC, 93–94
Ericsson, K. A., 32
Ethnic studies, 7
Executive control, of expert learners, 35
Expert learners, 31–32; and assessment, 38; comprehension monitoring by, 33–34; executive control of, 35; and instruction, 35–38; knowledge of, 32–33; motivation of, 34–35. *See also* Lifelong learning

Farr, M. J., 31, 32
Farris, E., 60
Feltovich, P. J., 32
Fersh, S. H., 100
Fideler, E. F., 13, 14, 19
50 Hours: A Core Curriculum for College Students, 52, 95
Finn, C. E., Jr., 93
Ford Foundation, 1
Franke, T. L., 2, 59, 66
Fredrickson, J., 2, 67, 73
Freshmen: at community colleges, 1; parallel year for, 7
Functional values, 43

Gaff, J. G., 1, 2, 5, 12, 22, 23, 65, 69, 89, 97
Gainer, L. J., 31, 77
Gender studies, 7
General education, 1–2; approaches to, 21; at community colleges, 1; in curriculum, 5–6; and developmental education, 59–65; globalized, 2, 54–58, 99–101; and habits of thought, 28–29; Michigan study of, 13–19; and occupational education, 26–27, 86–90; for part-time, nondegree students, 23–24; readings on, 94–102; reform in, 6–11; and workplace, 81–83
Geography, world, 57
Gick, M. L., 36
Glaser, R., 31, 32
Globalization: of cultural literacy, 52; of general education curriculum, 7, 54–58, 99–101
Glock, N. C., 100
Gobbo, C., 32
Goodwin, D., 80
Greenfield, R. K., 96
Griffith, M., 61, 62

Habits of thought, cultivation of, 28–29
Hamline University, 10
Harlacher, E. L., 98
Harvard, 60
Higginbottom, G. H., 98
Hirsch, E. D., Jr., 52, 93
History, as shared use of time, 71. *See also* Western civilization; World civilizations
Holland, S. I., 31
Holyoak, K. J., 36
Hopkins, S., 62
Hsiao, K. P., 3, 93, 102
Humanities, 94–95, 101, 102; and occupational education, 86–91

Illinois Community College Board, 77
Indoctrination, 45, 50; direct, 45, 50; rationalized, 45, 50
Institutions, shared membership in, 69
Instruction, and expert learner findings, 35–38. *See also* Teaching
Iowa State College, 59–60

Jackson State University, 70

Jacobs, B., 61, 62, 75, 84
Jacobs, J., 2, 76, 77, 78
Johnson, B. L., 21, 23, 93
Johnson County Community College, 69, 97
Judy, J. E., 32

Kalamazoo Valley Community College, 89, 90
Karabel, J., 1, 80
Kazis, R., 75
Kerr, C., 22
King, J., 90
Kirkwood Community College, 89–90, 102
Klein, T., 97
Knowledge, of expert learners, 32–33
Kroe, E., 23

LaGuardia Community College, 11, 69
Laney College, Project Bridge at, 61–62
Lansing Community College, 56, 62–63
Larkin, J. H., 32
Learning, lifelong, 98–99. See also Expert learners
Learning and Study Strategies Inventory (LASSI), 38
Lemon, J., 101
Lesgold, A. M., 32
Levin, B. H., 1
Levine, A., 67, 68, 69, 70, 71
Liberal arts, 6, 10–11, 97–98
Lifelong learning, and general education, 98–99. See also Expert learners
Lipson, M. Y., 32, 34
Literature, study of, 60. See also Humanities
Los Medanos College, 11
Lukenbill, J. D., 70

McAlinden, S. P., 76, 79
McCabe, R., 9, 10
McCombs, B., 32
McDermott, J., 32
McNamara, L. L., 100
McNeill, W. H., 55
Majchrzak, A., 76
Mansfield, W., 60
Maricopa Writing Project, 68
Mathematics: in general and developmental education, 60; in globalized curriculum, 57

Matthews, R., 69
Maxwell, M., 59, 60
Mayhew, L. B., 1
Means, M. L., 32
Mehrens, W., 77
Meltzer, A. S., 31
Metacurriculum, 37–38
Miami-Dade, 10
Michigan Board of Education, 81
Michigan study, 13; approach and methodology of, 13–15; and general education, 18–19; results of, 15–18
Miles, C., 99
Minorities: curriculum for, 68–72; general education of, 67–68; and Western-based curriculum, 53. See also At-risk students
Mission: crisis of, 10; statement of, 18
Moral values, 42–43
Morris, D., 31
Motivation, of expert learners, 34–35

National Council for Occupational Education, 86
National Endowment for the Humanities (NEH), 52, 89, 94; and study of civilizations, 52–53, 54
National Issues Forums, 63
National Longitudinal Study of the High School Graduating Class of 1972, 23
National Technical Institute for the Deaf, 69
Nature, shared relationship with, 70–71
New Jersey Basic Skills Council, 60
Nolte, W. H., 101
North Seattle Community College, 72
Northern New Mexico Community College, 101

Oakton Community College, 11
Oberlin College, 60
Occupational education: in community colleges, 26–27; and general education, 86–90, 101–102; and humanities, 90–91. See also Vocational education
Ottinger, C. A., 53

Palmer, D. R., 38
Paris, S. G., 32, 34
Parler, N. P., 71

Perkins, D. R., 101
Personal welfare values, 43
Phelps, L. A., 78
Piore, M. J., 79, 80
Political values, 43
Polson, P. G., 32
Posner, M. I., 32
Production and consumption, shared, 69–70
Prof-Scam: Professors and the Demise of Higher Education (Sykes), 93
Project Bridge, 61–62

Quality, and access, 9

Raisman, N. A., 2, 3, 13, 16, 18, 20, 93, 97, 102
Ravitch, D., 93
Rees, E., 32
Rendón, L. I., 2, 67, 73
Rochester Community College, 11
Roueche, J. E., 68
Roueche, S. D., 68

Sabel, C. F., 79, 80
Saunders, W. S., 99
Schoolcraft College, 62
Schulte, A. C., 38
Schunk, D. H., 34, 35
Schuster, J. H., 93
Science, in globalized curriculum, 57
Scientific values, 43
Self-regulated learners. *See* Expert learners
Sessions, R., 89, 102
Shared Vision Task Force, 64, 86, 90
Shaw, R. G., 69, 70, 72
Simon, D. P., 32
Simon, H. A., 32
Sjoquist, D. P., 2, 51, 56, 58
Skills: fundamental, 6; general and vocational education, 78–80; needed by business, 75–76; and workplace, 76–78
Smith, A., 31
Smith, V., 6
Social-conventional values, 43
Southern Maine Technical College, 88, 90
Spain, L., 100
Steck, D. E., 56

Stone, G.V.M., 2, 31, 39
Student choice, doctrine of, 24–25
Students: assessing acquisition of values by, 49–50; at-risk, 36; need for active, 8–9; part-time, nondegree, 23–24. *See also* Minorities
Sykes, C. J., 93

Teaching, of values, 41, 44–49, 50. *See also* Instruction
Technical values, 43
Texas, University of, learning skills class at, 36–38
Third Wave civilization, 51
Thomas, R. M., 2, 41, 50
Thomas, T. R., 101
Toffler, A., 51
Tougaloo College, 10
Training: customized courses for, 77; union-management courses for, 77–78. *See also* Vocational education
Transfer function, 1, 10, 96
Turiel, E., 42
Tuskegee Institute, 71

University Microfilm International Articles Clearinghouse, 94
Utah Valley Community College, 98

Valencia Community College, 100
Values, 7; assessing students' acquisition of, 49–50; choosing methods for teaching, 44; intentional teaching of, 44–47; nature of, 41–42; shared, 71–72; and stated criteria, 47–49; by subject matter fields, 43–44; types of, 42–43
Values clarification, 45–46, 50
Van Mater Stone, G., 2, 31, 39
Vaughan, G. B., 98
Vocational education: and academic education, 75; crisis in, 80–81; and general education, 78–83, 101–102; and liberal arts, 10–11; and training, 77–78. *See also* Occupational education
Voss, J. F., 32

Weinstein, C. E., 2, 31, 35, 38, 39
Western civilization, study of, 52–54
What Do Our 17-Year-Olds Know (Ravitch and Finn), 93
Wiggins, G., 99

Wilson, S., 61, 62
Winona State College, 11
Wixson, K. K., 32, 34
Wood, M. T., 64
Workplace: and general education, 81–83; skills needed in, 76–78

World civilizations, courses on, 54–56
Writing, 60; across the curriculum, 63, 68

Zimmerman, B. J., 34, 35
Zwerling, L. S., 1

Ordering Information

New Directions for Community Colleges is a series of paperback books that provides expert assistance to help community colleges meet the challenges of their distinctive and expanding educational mission. Books in the series are published quarterly in spring, summer, fall, and winter and are available for purchase by subscription as well as by single copy.

Subscriptions for 1993 cost $48.00 for individuals (a savings of 20 percent over single-copy prices) and $70.00 for institutions, agencies, and libraries. Please do not send institutional checks for personal subscriptions. Standing orders are accepted.

Single copies cost $15.95 when payment accompanies order. (California, New Jersey, New York, and Washington, D.C., residents please include appropriate sales tax.) Billed orders will be charged postage and handling.

Discounts for quantity orders are available. Please write to the address below for information.

All orders must include either the name of an individual or an official purchase order number. Please submit your order as follows:
    Subscriptions: specify series and year subscription is to begin
    Single copies: include individual title code (such as CC1)

Mail all orders to:
    Jossey-Bass Publishers
    350 Sansome Street
    San Francisco, California 94104

CC80 First-Generation Students: Confronting the Cultural Issues, L. Steven Zwerling,
Howard B. London
CC79 Maintaining Faculty Excellence, Keith Kroll
CC78 Prisoners of Elitism: The Community College's Struggle for Stature,
Billie Wright Dziech, William R. Vilter
CC77 Critical Thinking: Educational Imperative, Cynthia A. Barnes
CC76 Enhancing Teaching and Administration Through Scholarship,
George B. Vaughan, James C. Palmer
CC75 Economic and Work Force Development, Geneva Waddell
CC74 Rekindling Minority Enrollment, Dan Angel, Adriana Barrera
CC73 Writing Across the Curriculum in Community Colleges, Linda C. Stanley,
Joanna Ambron
CC72 Models for Conducting Institutional Research, Peter R. MacDougall,
Jack Friedlander
CC71 The Role of the Learning Resource Center in Instruction, Margaret Holleman
CC70 Developing International Education Programs, Richard K. Greenfield
CC69 The Viability of the Private Junior College, Robert H. Woodroof
CC68 Alternative Funding Sources, James L. Catanzaro, Allen D. Arnold
CC67 Perspectives on Student Development, William L. Deegan, Terry O'Banion
CC66 Using Student Tracking Systems Effectively, Trudy H. Bers
CC65 A Search for Institutional Distinctiveness, Barbara K. Townsend
CC64 External Influences on the Curriculum, David B. Wolf, Mary Lou Zoglin
CC63 Collaborating with High Schools, Janet E. Lieberman
CC62 Issues in Personnel Management, Richard I. Miller, Edward W. Holzapfel, Jr.
CC60 Marketing Strategies for Changing Times, Wellford W. Wilms, Richard W. Moore
CC58 Developing Occupational Programs, Charles R. Doty
CC57 Teaching the Developmental Education Student, Kenneth M. Ahrendt